SUSE Manager API Documentation

SUSE Manager 3.1

SUSE Manager 3.1

Welcome to the SUSE Manager API. By using the included API calls, you can easily automate many of the tasks you perform everyday. All API calls are grouped by common functionality.

Publication Date: 11/23/2017

SUSE LLC
10 Canal Park Drive
Suite 200
Cambridge MA 02141
USA
https://www.suse.com/documentation ↗

Contents

Sample Scripts xxxv

Frequently Asked Questions xxxvii

1   actionchain 1

1.1   addConfigurationDeployment 1

1.2   addErrataUpdate 1

1.3   addPackageInstall 2

1.4   addPackageRemoval 2

1.5   addPackageUpgrade 3

1.6   addPackageVerify 3

1.7   addScriptRun 4

1.8   addScriptRun 4

1.9   addSystemReboot 5

1.10   createChain 5

1.11   deleteChain 6

1.12   listChainActions 6

1.13   listChains 7

1.14   removeAction 7

1.15   renameChain 8

1.16   scheduleChain 8

2   activationkey 9

2.1   addChildChannels 9

2.2   addConfigChannels 9

2.3   addEntitlements 10

2.4   addPackageNames 11

2.5   addPackages 11

2.6   addServerGroups 12

2.7   checkConfigDeployment 12

2.8   clone 13

2.9   create 13

2.10   create 14

2.11   delete 14

2.12   disableConfigDeployment 15

2.13   enableConfigDeployment 15

2.14   getDetails 16

2.15   listActivatedSystems 17

2.16   listActivationKeys 17

2.17   listChannels 19

2.18   listConfigChannels 19

2.19   removeChildChannels 20

2.20   removeConfigChannels 21

2.21   removeEntitlements 21

2.22   removePackageNames 22

2.23   removePackages 22

2.24   removeServerGroups 23

2.25   setConfigChannels 23

2.26   setDetails 24

3   api 26

3.1   getApiCallList 26

3.2   getApiNamespaceCallList 26

3.3   getApiNamespaces 27

3.4   getVersion 27

3.5   systemVersion 27

4   audit 29

4.1   listImagesByPatchStatus 29

4.2   listImagesByPatchStatus 30

4.3   listSystemsByPatchStatus 31

4.4   listSystemsByPatchStatus 32

5   auth 34

5.1   login 34

5.2   login 34

5.3   logout 35

6   channel 36

6.1   listAllChannels 36

6.2   listManageableChannels 36

6.3   listMyChannels 37

6.4   listPopularChannels 38

6.5   listRedHatChannels 38

6.6   `listRetiredChannels` 39

6.7   `listSharedChannels` 40

6.8   `listSoftwareChannels` 40

6.9   `listVendorChannels` 41

7   channel.access 42

7.1   `disableUserRestrictions` 42

7.2   `enableUserRestrictions` 42

7.3   `getOrgSharing` 42

7.4   `setOrgSharing` 43

8   channel.org 44

8.1   `disableAccess` 44

8.2   `enableAccess` 44

8.3   `list` 45

9   channel.software 46

9.1   `addPackages` 46

9.2   `addRepoFilter` 46

9.3   `associateRepo` 47

9.4   `clearRepoFilters` 48

9.5   `clone` 48

9.6   `create` 49

9.7   `create` 50

9.8   `create` 51

9.9   `createRepo` 51

9.10   `createRepo` 52

9.11   `createRepo` 53

9.12   `delete` 54

9.13   `disassociateRepo` 54

9.14   `getChannelLastBuildById` 55

9.15   `getDetails` 56

9.16   `getDetails` 57

9.17   `getRepoDetails` 58

9.18   `getRepoDetails` 59

9.19   `getRepoSyncCronExpression` 59

9.20   `isGloballySubscribable` 60

9.21   `isUserManageable` 60

9.22   `isUserSubscribable` 61

9.23   `listAllPackages` 61

9.24   `listAllPackages` 62

9.25   `listAllPackages` 63

9.26   `listAllPackages` 63

9.27   `listAllPackages` 64

9.28   `listAllPackagesByDate` 65

9.29   `listAllPackagesByDate` 66

9.30   `listAllPackagesByDate` 67

9.31   `listArches` 67

9.32   `listChannelRepos` 68

9.33   `listChildren` 69

9.34   `listErrata` 70

9.35   listErrata 71

9.36   listErrata 71

9.37   listErrata 72

9.38   listErrata 73

9.39   listErrata 73

9.40   listErrataByType 74

9.41   listErrataNeedingSync 75

9.42   listLatestPackages 76

9.43   listPackagesWithoutChannel 76

9.44   listRepoFilters 77

9.45   listSubscribedSystems 78

9.46   listSystemChannels 78

9.47   listUserRepos 79

9.48   mergeErrata 79

9.49   mergeErrata 80

9.50   mergeErrata 80

9.51   mergePackages 81

9.52   regenerateNeededCache 82

9.53   regenerateNeededCache 82

9.54   regenerateYumCache 83

9.55   removeErrata 83

9.56   removePackages 84

9.57   removeRepo 84

9.58   removeRepo 84

9.59   removeRepoFilter 85

9.60   setContactDetails 85

9.61   setDetails 86

9.62   setGloballySubscribable 86

9.63   setRepoFilters 87

9.64   setSystemChannels 87

9.65   setUserManageable 88

9.66   setUserSubscribable 88

9.67   subscribeSystem 89

9.68   syncErrata 90

9.69   syncRepo 90

9.70   syncRepo 91

9.71   syncRepo 91

9.72   syncRepo 92

9.73   syncRepo 92

9.74   updateRepo 93

9.75   updateRepoLabel 93

9.76   updateRepoLabel 94

9.77   updateRepoSsl 95

9.78   updateRepoSsl 96

9.79   updateRepoUrl 97

9.80   updateRepoUrl 97

10   configchannel 99

10.1   channelExists 99

10.2   create 99

10.3   createOrUpdatePath 100

10.4   createOrUpdateSymlink 102

10.5   deleteChannels 103

10.6   deleteFileRevisions 103

10.7   deleteFiles 104

10.8   deployAllSystems 104

10.9   deployAllSystems 105

10.10   deployAllSystems 105

10.11   deployAllSystems 106

10.12   getDetails 106

10.13   getDetails 107

10.14   getEncodedFileRevision 108

10.15   getFileRevision 109

10.16   getFileRevisions 110

10.17   listFiles 111

10.18   listGlobals 112

10.19   listSubscribedSystems 113

10.20   lookupChannelInfo 113

10.21   lookupFileInfo 114

10.22   lookupFileInfo 115

10.23   scheduleFileComparisons 116

10.24   update 117

11 distchannel 119

11.1 listDefaultMaps 119

11.2 listMapsForOrg 119

11.3 listMapsForOrg 120

11.4 setMapForOrg 120

12 errata 122

12.1 addPackages 122

12.2 applicableToChannels 122

12.3 bugzillaFixes 123

12.4 clone 123

12.5 cloneAsOriginal 124

12.6 cloneAsOriginalAsync 125

12.7 cloneAsync 125

12.8 create 126

12.9 delete 127

12.10 findByCve 128

12.11 getDetails 128

12.12 listAffectedSystems 129

12.13 listByDate 130

12.14 listCves 130

12.15 listKeywords 131

12.16 listPackages 131

12.17 listUnpublishedErrata 132

12.18 publish 133

12.19   publishAsOriginal 133

12.20   removePackages 134

12.21   setDetails 135

13   formula 137

13.1   getCombinedFormulasByServerId 137

13.2   getFormulasByGroupId 137

13.3   getFormulasByServerId 138

13.4   listFormulas 138

13.5   setFormulasOfGroup 139

13.6   setFormulasOfServer 139

14   image 141

14.1   delete 141

14.2   getCustomValues 141

14.3   getDetails 142

14.4   getRelevantErrata 143

14.5   importImage 143

14.6   listImages 144

14.7   listPackages 144

14.8   scheduleImageBuild 145

15   image.profile 146

15.1   create 146

15.2   delete 146

15.3   deleteCustomValues 147

15.4   getCustomValues 147

15.5   getDetails 148

15.6   listImageProfileTypes 148

15.7   listImageProfiles 149

15.8   setCustomValues 149

15.9   setDetails 150

16   image.store 151

16.1   create 151

16.2   delete 151

16.3   getDetails 152

16.4   listImageStoreTypes 152

16.5   listImageStores 153

16.6   setDetails 153

17   kickstart 155

17.1   cloneProfile 155

17.2   createProfile 155

17.3   createProfile 156

17.4   createProfileWithCustomUrl 156

17.5   createProfileWithCustomUrl 157

17.6   deleteProfile 157

17.7   disableProfile 158

17.8   findKickstartForIp 158

17.9   importFile 159

17.10   importFile 159

17.11   importFile 160

17.12   importRawFile 161

17.13   importRawFile 161

17.14   isProfileDisabled 162

17.15   listAllIpRanges 162

17.16   listAutoinstallableChannels 163

17.17   listKickstartableChannels 164

17.18   listKickstartableTrees 165

17.19   listKickstarts 166

17.20   renameProfile 166

18   kickstart.filepreservation 168

18.1   create 168

18.2   delete 168

18.3   getDetails 169

18.4   listAllFilePreservations 169

19   kickstart.keys 171

19.1   create 171

19.2   delete 171

19.3   getDetails 171

19.4   listAllKeys 172

19.5   update 172

20   kickstart.profile 174

20.1   addIpRange 174

20.2   addScript 174

20.3   addScript 175

20.4   addScript 175

20.5   compareActivationKeys 176

20.6   compareAdvancedOptions 178

20.7   comparePackages 179

20.8   downloadKickstart 180

20.9   downloadRenderedKickstart 180

20.10   getAdvancedOptions 181

20.11   getAvailableRepositories 181

20.12   getCfgPreservation 182

20.13   getChildChannels 182

20.14   getCustomOptions 183

20.15   getKickstartTree 183

20.16   getRepositories 184

20.17   getUpdateType 184

20.18   getVariables 184

20.19   getVirtualizationType 185

20.20   listIpRanges 185

20.21   listScripts 186

20.22   orderScripts 187

20.23   removeIpRange 187

20.24   removeScript 188

20.25   setAdvancedOptions 188

20.26   setCfgPreservation 189

20.27   setChildChannels 190

20.28   setCustomOptions 190

20.29   setKickstartTree 190

20.30   setLogging 191

20.31   setRepositories 191

20.32   setUpdateType 192

20.33   setVariables 192

20.34   setVirtualizationType 193

21   kickstart.profile.keys 194

21.1   addActivationKey 194

21.2   getActivationKeys 194

21.3   removeActivationKey 195

22   kickstart.profile.software 197

22.1   appendToSoftwareList 197

22.2   getSoftwareDetails 197

22.3   getSoftwareList 198

22.4   setSoftwareDetails 198

22.5   setSoftwareList 199

22.6   setSoftwareList 199

23   kickstart.profile.system 200

23.1   addFilePreservations 200

23.2   addKeys 200

23.3   checkConfigManagement 201

23.4   checkRemoteCommands 201

23.5   disableConfigManagement 202

23.6   disableRemoteCommands 202

23.7   enableConfigManagement 203

23.8   enableRemoteCommands 203

23.9   getLocale 203

23.10   getPartitioningScheme 204

23.11   getRegistrationType 204

23.12   getSELinux 205

23.13   listFilePreservations 205

23.14   listKeys 206

23.15   removeFilePreservations 206

23.16   removeKeys 207

23.17   setLocale 207

23.18   setPartitioningScheme 208

23.19   setRegistrationType 208

23.20   setSELinux 209

24   kickstart.snippet 210

24.1   createOrUpdate 210

24.2   delete 210

24.3   listAll 211

24.4   listCustom 211

24.5   listDefault 212

25   kickstart.tree 213

25.1   create 213

25.2   delete 213

25.3   deleteTreeAndProfiles 214

25.4   getDetails 214

25.5   list 215

25.6   listInstallTypes 215

25.7   rename 216

25.8   update 216

26   org 217

26.1   create 217

26.2   delete 218

26.3   getCrashFileSizeLimit 218

26.4   getDetails 218

26.5   getDetails 219

26.6   getPolicyForScapFileUpload 220

26.7   getPolicyForScapResultDeletion 220

26.8   isCrashReportingEnabled 221

26.9   isCrashfileUploadEnabled 221

26.10   isErrataEmailNotifsForOrg 222

26.11   isOrgConfigManagedByOrgAdmin 222

26.12   listOrgs 223

26.13   listUsers 224

26.14   migrateSystems 224

26.15   setCrashFileSizeLimit 225

26.16   setCrashReporting 225

26.17   setCrashfileUpload 226

26.18   setErrataEmailNotifsForOrg 226

26.19   setOrgConfigManagedByOrgAdmin 227

26.20   setPolicyForScapFileUpload 227

26.21   setPolicyForScapResultDeletion 228

26.22   updateName 228

27   org.trusts 230

27.1   addTrust 230

27.2   getDetails 230

27.3   listChannelsConsumed 231

27.4   listChannelsProvided 231

27.5   listOrgs 232

27.6   listSystemsAffected 232

27.7   listTrusts 233

27.8   removeTrust 233

28   packages 235

28.1   findByNvrea 235

28.2   getDetails 236

28.3   getPackage 237

28.4   getPackageUrl 237

28.5   listChangelog 237

28.6   listDependencies 238

28.7   listFiles 239

28.8   listProvidingChannels 239

28.9   listProvidingErrata 240

28.10   listSourcePackages 240

28.11   removePackage 241

28.12   removeSourcePackage 241

29   packages.provider 242

29.1   associateKey 242

29.2   list 242

29.3   listKeys 243

30   packages.search 244

30.1   advanced 244

30.2   advancedWithActKey 245

30.3   advancedWithChannel 246

30.4   name 247

30.5   nameAndDescription 247

30.6   nameAndSummary 248

31   preferences.locale 250

31.1   listLocales 250

31.2   listTimeZones 250

31.3   setLocale 251

31.4   setTimeZone 251

32   proxy 252

32.1   activateProxy 252

32.2   createMonitoringScout 252

32.3   deactivateProxy 252

32.4   isProxy 253

32.5 listAvailableProxyChannels 253

33 satellite 254

33.1 isMonitoringEnabled 254

33.2 isMonitoringEnabledBySystemId 254

33.3 listProxies 254

34 schedule 256

34.1 archiveActions 256

34.2 cancelActions 256

34.3 deleteActions 257

34.4 failSystemAction 257

34.5 failSystemAction 258

34.6 listAllActions 258

34.7 listArchivedActions 259

34.8 listCompletedActions 259

34.9 listCompletedSystems 260

34.10 listFailedActions 261

34.11 listFailedSystems 261

34.12 listInProgressActions 262

34.13 listInProgressSystems 263

34.14 rescheduleActions 263

35 subscriptionmatching.pinnedsubscription 265

35.1 create 265

35.2 delete 265

35.3 list 266

36   sync.content 267

36.1   addChannel 267

36.2   addCredentials 267

36.3   deleteCredentials 268

36.4   listChannels 268

36.5   listCredentials 269

36.6   listProducts 269

36.7   synchronizeChannelFamilies 271

36.8   synchronizeChannels 272

36.9   synchronizeProductChannels 272

36.10   synchronizeProducts 273

36.11   synchronizeSubscriptions 273

37   sync.master 274

37.1   addToMaster 274

37.2   create 274

37.3   delete 275

37.4   getDefaultMaster 275

37.5   getMaster 276

37.6   getMasterByLabel 276

37.7   getMasterOrgs 277

37.8   getMasters 277

37.9   hasMaster 278

37.10   makeDefault 278

37.11   mapToLocal 278

37.12 setCaCert 279

37.13 setMasterOrgs 279

37.14 unsetDefaultMaster 280

37.15 update 280

38 sync.slave 282

38.1 create 282

38.2 delete 282

38.3 getAllowedOrgs 283

38.4 getSlave 283

38.5 getSlaveByName 284

38.6 getSlaves 284

38.7 setAllowedOrgs 285

38.8 update 285

39 system 287

39.1 addEntitlements 287

39.2 addNote 287

39.3 applyErrata 288

39.4 bootstrap 288

39.5 bootstrap 289

39.6 comparePackageProfile 289

39.7 comparePackages 290

39.8 createPackageProfile 291

39.9 createSystemRecord 291

39.10 createSystemRecord 292

39.11 deleteCustomValues 292

39.12 deleteGuestProfiles 293

39.13 deleteNote 293

39.14 deleteNotes 294

39.15 deletePackageProfile 294

39.16 deleteSystem 295

39.17 deleteSystem 295

39.18 deleteSystems 295

39.19 deleteTagFromSnapshot 296

39.20 downloadSystemId 296

39.21 getConnectionPath 297

39.22 getCpu 297

39.23 getCustomValues 298

39.24 getDetails 298

39.25 getDevices 300

39.26 getDmi 300

39.27 getEntitlements 301

39.28 getEventHistory 301

39.29 getId 302

39.30 getInstalledProducts 303

39.31 getKernelLivePatch 303

39.32 getMemory 304

39.33 getName 304

39.34 getNetwork 305

39.35 getNetworkDevices 305

39.36 getOsaPing 306

39.37 getRegistrationDate 307

39.38 getRelevantErrata 307

39.39 getRelevantErrataByType 308

39.40 getRunningKernel 308

39.41 getScriptActionDetails 309

39.42 getScriptResults 310

39.43 getSubscribedBaseChannel 310

39.44 getSystemCurrencyMultipliers 311

39.45 getSystemCurrencyScores 312

39.46 getUnscheduledErrata 312

39.47 getUuid 313

39.48 getVariables 313

39.49 isNvreInstalled 314

39.50 isNvreInstalled 314

39.51 listActivationKeys 315

39.52 listActiveSystems 315

39.53 listActiveSystemsDetails 316

39.54 listAdministrators 318

39.55 listAllInstallablePackages 319

39.56 listBaseChannels 319

39.57 listChildChannels 320

39.58 listDuplicatesByHostname 321

39.59 listDuplicatesByIp 321

39.60 listDuplicatesByMac 322

39.61 listExtraPackages 323

39.62 listGroups 323

39.63 listInactiveSystems 324

39.64 listInactiveSystems 325

39.65 listLatestAvailablePackage 325

39.66 listLatestInstallablePackages 326

39.67 listLatestUpgradablePackages 327

39.68 listMigrationTargets 328

39.69 listNewerInstalledPackages 328

39.70 listNotes 329

39.71 listOlderInstalledPackages 330

39.72 listOutOfDateSystems 330

39.73 listPackageProfiles 331

39.74 listPackages 332

39.75 listPackagesFromChannel 332

39.76 listPhysicalSystems 333

39.77 listSubscribableBaseChannels 334

39.78 listSubscribableChildChannels 334

39.79 listSubscribedChildChannels 335

39.80 listSuggestedReboot 336

39.81 listSystemEvents 337

39.82 listSystemEvents 338

39.83   listSystems 340

39.84   listSystemsWithExtraPackages 341

39.85   listSystemsWithPackage 341

39.86   listSystemsWithPackage 342

39.87   listUngroupedSystems 343

39.88   listUserSystems 343

39.89   listUserSystems 344

39.90   listVirtualGuests 345

39.91   listVirtualHosts 345

39.92   obtainReactivationKey 346

39.93   obtainReactivationKey 346

39.94   provisionSystem 347

39.95   provisionSystem 347

39.96   provisionVirtualGuest 348

39.97   provisionVirtualGuest 348

39.98   provisionVirtualGuest 349

39.99   removeEntitlements 349

39.100   scheduleApplyErrata 350

39.101   scheduleApplyErrata 350

39.102   scheduleApplyErrata 351

39.103   scheduleApplyErrata 352

39.104   scheduleCertificateUpdate 352

39.105   scheduleCertificateUpdate 353

39.106   scheduleDistUpgrade 353

39.107   scheduleGuestAction 354

39.108   scheduleGuestAction 354

39.109   scheduleHardwareRefresh 355

39.110   schedulePackageInstall 355

39.111   schedulePackageInstall 356

39.112   schedulePackageInstallByNevra 356

39.113   schedulePackageInstallByNevra 357

39.114   schedulePackageRefresh 358

39.115   schedulePackageRemove 358

39.116   schedulePackageRemove 359

39.117   schedulePackageRemoveByNevra 359

39.118   schedulePackageRemoveByNevra 360

39.119   scheduleReboot 361

39.120   scheduleSPMigration 361

39.121   scheduleSPMigration 362

39.122   scheduleScriptRun 362

39.123   scheduleScriptRun 363

39.124   scheduleScriptRun 364

39.125   scheduleScriptRun 364

39.126   scheduleSyncPackagesWithSystem 365

39.127   searchByName 365

39.128   sendOsaPing 366

39.129   setBaseChannel 366

39.130   setBaseChannel 367

39.131 setChildChannels 367

39.132 setCustomValues 368

39.133 setDetails 368

39.134 setGroupMembership 369

39.135 setGuestCpus 370

39.136 setGuestMemory 370

39.137 setLockStatus 371

39.138 setPrimaryInterface 371

39.139 setProfileName 371

39.140 setVariables 372

39.141 tagLatestSnapshot 373

39.142 unentitle 373

39.143 upgradeEntitlement 374

39.144 whoRegistered 374

40   system.config 376

40.1   addChannels 376

40.2   createOrUpdatePath 377

40.3   createOrUpdateSymlink 379

40.4   deleteFiles 380

40.5   deployAll 381

40.6   listChannels 381

40.7   listFiles 382

40.8   lookupFileInfo 383

40.9   removeChannels 384

40.10   setChannels 385

41   system.crash 386

41.1   createCrashNote 386

41.2   deleteCrash 386

41.3   deleteCrashNote 386

41.4   getCrashCountInfo 387

41.5   getCrashFile 387

41.6   getCrashFileUrl 388

41.7   getCrashNotesForCrash 388

41.8   getCrashOverview 389

41.9   getCrashesByUuid 389

41.10   listSystemCrashFiles 390

41.11   listSystemCrashes 390

42   system.custominfo 392

42.1   createKey 392

42.2   deleteKey 392

42.3   listAllKeys 392

42.4   updateKey 393

43   system.provisioning.snapshot 394

43.1   addTagToSnapshot 394

43.2   deleteSnapshot 394

43.3   deleteSnapshots 394

43.4   deleteSnapshots 395

43.5   listSnapshotConfigFiles 396

43.6   listSnapshotPackages 397

43.7   listSnapshots 398

43.8   rollbackToSnapshot 399

43.9   rollbackToTag 399

43.10 rollbackToTag 400

44   system.scap 401

44.1   deleteXccdfScan 401

44.2   getXccdfScanDetails 401

44.3   getXccdfScanRuleResults 402

44.4   listXccdfScans 402

44.5   scheduleXccdfScan 403

44.6   scheduleXccdfScan 403

44.7   scheduleXccdfScan 404

44.8   scheduleXccdfScan 404

45   system.search 406

45.1   deviceDescription 406

45.2   deviceDriver 406

45.3   deviceId 407

45.4   deviceVendorId 408

45.5   hostname 408

45.6   ip 409

45.7   nameAndDescription 410

45.8   uuid 410

46 systemgroup 412

46.1 addOrRemoveAdmins 412

46.2 addOrRemoveSystems 412

46.3 create 413

46.4 delete 413

46.5 getDetails 414

46.6 getDetails 414

46.7 listActiveSystemsInGroup 415

46.8 listAdministrators 415

46.9 listAllGroups 416

46.10 listGroupsWithNoAssociatedAdmins 416

46.11 listInactiveSystemsInGroup 417

46.12 listInactiveSystemsInGroup 417

46.13 listSystems 418

46.14 listSystemsMinimal 419

46.15 scheduleApplyErrataToActive 420

46.16 scheduleApplyErrataToActive 420

46.17 update 421

47 user 422

47.1 addAssignedSystemGroup 422

47.2 addAssignedSystemGroups 422

47.3 addDefaultSystemGroup 423

47.4 addDefaultSystemGroups 423

47.5 addRole 424

47.6   create 424

47.7   create 425

47.8   delete 425

47.9   disable 426

47.10   enable 426

47.11   getCreateDefaultSystemGroup 426

47.12   getDetails 427

47.13   getLoggedInTime 428

47.14   listAssignableRoles 428

47.15   listAssignedSystemGroups 428

47.16   listDefaultSystemGroups 429

47.17   listRoles 430

47.18   listUsers 430

47.19   removeAssignedSystemGroup 431

47.20   removeAssignedSystemGroups 431

47.21   removeDefaultSystemGroup 432

47.22   removeDefaultSystemGroups 432

47.23   removeRole 433

47.24   setCreateDefaultSystemGroup 433

47.25   setDetails 434

47.26   setErrataNotifications 434

47.27   setReadOnly 435

47.28   usePamAuthentication 435

48   user.external 437

48.1   createExternalGroupToRoleMap 437

48.2   createExternalGroupToSystemGroupMap 438

48.3   deleteExternalGroupToRoleMap 438

48.4   deleteExternalGroupToSystemGroupMap 439

48.5   getDefaultOrg 439

48.6   getExternalGroupToRoleMap 439

48.7   getExternalGroupToSystemGroupMap 440

48.8   getKeepTemporaryRoles 440

48.9   getUseOrgUnit 441

48.10   listExternalGroupToRoleMaps 441

48.11   listExternalGroupToSystemGroupMaps 442

48.12   setDefaultOrg 442

48.13   setExternalGroupRoles 443

48.14   setExternalGroupSystemGroups 443

48.15   setKeepTemporaryRoles 444

48.16   setUseOrgUnit 444

49   virtualhostmanager 446

49.1   create 446

49.2   delete 446

49.3   getDetail 447

49.4   getModuleParameters 447

49.5   listAvailableVirtualHostGathererModules 448

49.6   listVirtualHostManagers 448

Sample Scripts

EXAMPLE 1: PERL EXAMPLE

This Perl example shows the `system.listUserSystems` call being used to get a list of systems a user has access to. In the example below, the name of each system will be printed.

```perl
#!/usr/bin/perl
use Frontier::Client;

my $HOST = 'manager.example.com';
my $user = 'username';
my $pass = 'password';

my $client = new Frontier::Client(url => "http://$HOST/rpc/api");
my $session = $client->call('auth.login',$user, $pass);

my $systems = $client->call('system.listUserSystems', $session);
foreach my $system (@$systems) {
    print $system->{'name'}."\n";
}
$client->call('auth.logout', $session);
```

EXAMPLE 2: PYTHON EXAMPLE

Below is an example of the `user.listUsers` call being used. Only the login of each user is printed.

```python
#!/usr/bin/python
import xmlrpclib

MANAGER_URL = "http://manager.example.com/rpc/api"
MANAGER_LOGIN = "username"
MANAGER_PASSWORD = "password"

client = xmlrpclib.Server(MANAGER_URL, verbose=0)

key = client.auth.login(MANAGER_LOGIN, MANAGER_PASSWORD)
list = client.user.list_users(key)
for user in list:
  print user.get('login')

client.auth.logout(key)
```

The following code shows how to use date-time parameters. This code will schedule immediate installation of package rhnlib-2.5.22.9.el6.noarch to system with id 1000000001.

```
#!/usr/bin/python
from datetime import datetime
import time
import xmlrpclib

MANAGER_URL = "http://manager.example.com/rpc/api"
MANAGER_LOGIN = "username"
MANAGER_PASSWORD = "password"

client = xmlrpclib.Server(MANAGER_URL, verbose=0)

key = client.auth.login(MANAGER_LOGIN, MANAGER_PASSWORD)
package_list = client.packages.findByNvrea(key, 'rhnlib', '2.5.22', '9.el6', '',
 'noarch')
today = datetime.today()
earliest_occurrence = xmlrpclib.DateTime(today)
client.system.schedulePackageInstall(key, 1000000001, package_list[0]['id'],
 earliest_occurrence)

client.auth.logout(key)
```

EXAMPLE 3: RUBY EXAMPLE

Below is an example of the `channel.listAllChannels` API call. List of channel labels
is printed.

```
#!/usr/bin/env ruby
require "xmlrpc/client"

@MANAGER_URL = "http://manager.example.com/rpc/api"
@MANAGER_LOGIN = "username"
@MANAGER_PASSWORD = "password"

@client = XMLRPC::Client.new2(@MANAGER_URL)

@key = @client.call('auth.login', @MANAGER_LOGIN, @MANAGER_PASSWORD)
channels = @client.call('channel.listAllChannels', @key)
for channel in channels do
    p channel["label"]
end

@client.call('auth.logout', @key)
```

Frequently Asked Questions

1. *What programming languages are supported by the SUSE Manager API?*

   Any language that provides an XMLRPC client interface will work with the SUSE Manager API. While Perl and Python are two of the most commonly used, an XMLRPC client implementation is available for every common language.

2. *When trying to call a specific function, the error "Fault returned from XML RPC Server, fault code -1: Could not find method METHOD in class..." is given. What is wrong?*

   Typically this is seen when either a function name is being called that doesn't exist, the number of parameters for a particular function is incorrect, or the type of a passed parameter is incorrect (Such as an array is expected, but a String is passed). Check all of these things.

3. *Should I call an API method using the naming scheme "methodName" or "method_name"?*

   Both of these are valid names for the same method, so use whichever you prefer.

1 actionchain

Provides the namespace for the Action Chain methods.

1.1 addConfigurationDeployment

Description

Adds an action to deploy a configuration file to an Action Chain.

Parameters

- string sessionKey - Session token, issued at login
- string chainLabel - Label of the chain
- int System ID - System ID
- array:

  - struct - config revision specifier

    - string "channelLabel" - Channel label
    - string "filePath" - Path of the configuration file
    - int "revision" - Revision number

Return Value

- int - 1 on success, exception thrown otherwise.

1.2 addErrataUpdate

Description

Adds Errata update to an Action Chain.

Parameters

- string sessionKey - Session token, issued at login
- int serverId - System ID

- array:

    - int - Errata ID
  - string chainLabel - Label of the chain

Return Value

  - int actionId - The action id of the scheduled action

1.3 addPackageInstall

Description

Adds package installation action to an Action Chain.

Parameters

  - string sessionKey - Session token, issued at login
  - int serverId - System ID
  - array:

    - int - Package ID
  - string chainLabel

Return Value

  - int - 1 on success, exception thrown otherwise.

1.4 addPackageRemoval

Description

Adds an action to remove installed packages on the system to an Action Chain.

Parameters

  - string sessionKey - Session token, issued at login
  - int serverId - System ID
  - array:

    - int - Package ID
  - string chainLabel - Label of the chain

Return Value

> * int actionId - The action id of the scheduled action or exception

1.5 addPackageUpgrade

Description

> Adds an action to upgrade installed packages on the system to an Action Chain.

Parameters

> * string sessionKey - Session token, issued at login
> * int serverId - System ID
> * array:
>
>   > * int - packageId
> * string chainLabel - Label of the chain

Return Value

> * int actionId - The id of the action or throw an exception

1.6 addPackageVerify

Description

> Adds an action to verify installed packages on the system to an Action Chain.

Parameters

> * string sessionKey - Session token, issued at login
> * int serverId - System ID
> * array:
>
>   > * int - packageId
> * string chainLabel - Label of the chain

Return Value

- int - 1 on success, exception thrown otherwise.

1.7 addScriptRun

Description

Add an action to run a script to an Action Chain. NOTE: The script body must be Base64 encoded!

Parameters

- string sessionKey - Session token, issued at login
- int serverId - System ID
- string chainLabel - Label of the chain
- string uid - User ID on the particular system
- string gid - Group ID on the particular system
- int timeout - Timeout
- string scriptBodyBase64 - Base64 encoded script body

Return Value

- int actionId - The id of the action or throw an exception

1.8 addScriptRun

Description

Add an action to run a script to an Action Chain. NOTE: The script body must be Base64 encoded!

Parameters

- string sessionKey - Session token, issued at login
- int serverId - System ID
- string chainLabel - Label of the chain
- string uid - User ID on the particular system
- string gid - Group ID on the particular system

- int timeout - Timeout
- string scriptBodyBase64 - Base64 encoded script body

Return Value

- int actionId - The id of the action or throw an exception

1.9 addSystemReboot

Description

Add system reboot to an Action Chain.

Parameters

- string sessionKey - Session token, issued at login
- int serverId
- string chainLabel - Label of the chain

Return Value

- int actionId - The action id of the scheduled action

1.10 createChain

Description

Create an Action Chain.

Parameters

- string sessionKey - Session token, issued at login
- string chainLabel - Label of the chain

Return Value

- int actionId - The ID of the created action chain

1.11 deleteChain

Description

Delete action chain by label.

Parameters

- string sessionKey - Session token, issued at login
- string chainLabel - Label of the chain

Return Value

- int - 1 on success, exception thrown otherwise.

1.12 listChainActions

Description

List all actions in the particular Action Chain.

Parameters

- string sessionKey - Session token, issued at login
- string chainLabel - Label of the chain

Return Value

- array:

  - struct - entry

    - int "id" - Action ID
    - string "label" - Label of an Action
    - string "created" - Created date/time

- string "earliest" - Earliest scheduled date/time
- string "type" - Type of the action
- string "modified" - Modified date/time
- string "cuid" - Creator UID

1.13 listChains

Description

List currently available action chains.

Parameters

- string sessionKey - Session token, issued at login

Return Value

- array:

  - struct - chain

    - string "label" - Label of an Action Chain
    - string "entrycount" - Number of entries in the Action Chain

1.14 removeAction

Description

Remove an action from an Action Chain.

Parameters

- string sessionKey - Session token, issued at login
- string chainLabel - Label of the chain
- int actionId - Action ID

Return Value

- int - 1 on success, exception thrown otherwise.

1.15   renameChain

Description

Rename an Action Chain.

Parameters

- string sessionKey - Session token, issued at login
- string previousLabel - Previous chain label
- string newLabel - New chain label

Return Value

- int - 1 on success, exception thrown otherwise.

1.16   scheduleChain

Description

Schedule the Action Chain so that its actions will actually occur.

Parameters

- string sessionKey - Session token, issued at login
- string chainLabel - Label of the chain
- dateTime.iso8601 Earliest date

Return Value

- int - 1 on success, exception thrown otherwise.

2 activationkey

Contains methods to access common activation key functions available from the web interface.

2.1 addChildChannels

Description

Add child channels to an activation key.

Parameters

- string sessionKey
- string key
- array:

    - string - childChannelLabel

Return Value

- int - 1 on success, exception thrown otherwise.

2.2 addConfigChannels

Description

Given a list of activation keys and configuration channels, this method adds given configuration channels to either the top or the bottom (whichever you specify) of an activation key's configuration channels list. The ordering of the configuration channels provided in the add list is maintained while adding. If one of the configuration channels in the 'add' list already exists in an activation key, the configuration channel will be re-ranked to the appropriate place.

Parameters

- string sessionKey
- array:

    - string - activationKey
- array:

    - string - List of configuration channel labels in the ranked order.
- boolean addToTop
    - true - To prepend the given channels to the beginning of the activation key's config channel list
    - false - To append the given channels to the end of the activation key's config channel list

Return Value

- int - 1 on success, exception thrown otherwise.

2.3 addEntitlements

Description

Add entitlements to an activation key. Currently only virtualization_host add-on entitlement is permitted.

Parameters

- string sessionKey
- string key
- array string - entitlement label

- virtualization_host

Return Value

- int - 1 on success, exception thrown otherwise.

2.4 addPackageNames

Description

Add packages to an activation key using package name only.

Deprecated - being replaced by addPackages(string sessionKey, string key, array[packages])

Available since: 10.2

Parameters

- string sessionKey
- string key
- array:

  - string - packageName

Return Value

- int - 1 on success, exception thrown otherwise.

2.5 addPackages

Description

Add packages to an activation key.

Parameters

- string sessionKey
- string key
- array:

  - struct - packages

- string "name" - Package name
- string "arch" - Arch label - Optional

Return Value

- int - 1 on success, exception thrown otherwise.

2.6 addServerGroups

Description

Add server groups to an activation key.

Parameters

- string sessionKey
- string key
- array:

    - int - serverGroupId

Return Value

- int - 1 on success, exception thrown otherwise.

2.7 checkConfigDeployment

Description

Check configuration file deployment status for the activation key specified.

Parameters

- string sessionKey
- string key

Return Value

- 1 if enabled, 0 if disabled, exception thrown otherwise.

2.8 clone

Description

Clone an existing activation key.

Parameters

- string sessionKey
- string key - Key to be cloned.
- string cloneDescription - Description of the cloned key.

Return Value

- string - The new activation key.

2.9 create

Description

Create a new activation key. The activation key parameter passed in will be prefixed with the organization ID, and this value will be returned from the create call. Eg. If the caller passes in the key "foo" and belong to an organization with the ID 100, the actual activation key will be "100-foo". This call allows for the setting of a usage limit on this activation key. If unlimited usage is desired see the similarly named API method with no usage limit argument.

Parameters

- string sessionKey
- string key - Leave empty to have new key autogenerated.
- string description
- string baseChannelLabel - Leave empty to accept default.
- int usageLimit - If unlimited usage is desired, use the create API that does not include the parameter.

- array string - Add-on entitlement label to associate with the key.

  - - virtualization_host
- boolean universalDefault

Return Value

- string - The new activation key.

2.10 create

Description

Create a new activation key with unlimited usage. The activation key parameter passed in will be prefixed with the organization ID, and this value will be returned from the create call. Eg. If the caller passes in the key "foo" and belong to an organization with the ID 100, the actual activation key will be "100-foo".

Parameters

- string sessionKey
- string key - Leave empty to have new key autogenerated.
- string description
- string baseChannelLabel - Leave empty to accept default.
- array string - Add-on entitlement label to associate with the key.

  - - virtualization_host
- boolean universalDefault

Return Value

- string - The new activation key.

2.11 delete

Description

Delete an activation key.

Parameters

- string sessionKey
- string key

Return Value

- int - 1 on success, exception thrown otherwise.

2.12 disableConfigDeployment

Description

Disable configuration file deployment for the specified activation key.

Parameters

- string sessionKey
- string key

Return Value

- int - 1 on success, exception thrown otherwise.

2.13 enableConfigDeployment

Description

Enable configuration file deployment for the specified activation key.

Parameters

- string sessionKey
- string key

Return Value

- int - 1 on success, exception thrown otherwise.

2.14 getDetails

Description

Lookup an activation key's details.

Available since: 10.2

Parameters

- string sessionKey
- string key

Return Value

- struct - activation key

    - string "key"
    - string "description"
    - int "usage_limit"
    - string "base_channel_label"
    - array "child_channel_labels"

        - string - childChannelLabel
    - array "entitlements"

        - string - entitlementLabel
    - array "server_group_ids"

        - string - serverGroupId
    - array "package_names"

        - string - packageName - (deprecated by packages)
    - array "packages"

        - struct - package

- string "name" - packageName
- string "arch" - archLabel - optional
- boolean "universal_default"
- boolean "disabled"
- string "contact_method" - One of the following:
  - default
  - ssh-push
  - ssh-push-tunnel

2.15 listActivatedSystems

Description

List the systems activated with the key provided.

Parameters

- string sessionKey
- string key

Return Value

- array:
  - struct - system structure
    - int "id" - System id
    - string "hostname"
    - dateTime.iso8601 "last_checkin" - Last time server successfully checked in

2.16 listActivationKeys

Description

List activation keys that are visible to the user.
Available since: 10.2

Parameters

- string sessionKey

Return Value

- array:

    - struct - activation key

        - string "key"
        - string "description"
        - int "usage_limit"
        - string "base_channel_label"
        - array "child_channel_labels"

            - string - childChannelLabel
        - array "entitlements"

            - string - entitlementLabel
        - array "server_group_ids"

            - string - serverGroupId
        - array "package_names"

            - string - packageName - (deprecated by packages)
        - array "packages"

            - struct - package

                - string "name" - packageName
                - string "arch" - archLabel - optional
        - boolean "universal_default"
        - boolean "disabled"

- string "contact_method" - One of the following:
  - default
  - ssh-push
  - ssh-push-tunnel

2.17 listChannels

Description

List the channels for the given activation key with temporary authentication tokens to access them. Authentication is done via a machine specific password.

Parameters

- string minionId - The id of the minion to authenticate with.
- string machinePassword - password specific to a machine.
- string activationKey - activation key to use channels from.

Return Value

- array:

  - struct - channelInfo

    - string "label" - Channel label
    - string "name" - Channel name
    - string "url" - Channel url
    - string "token" - Channel access token

2.18 listConfigChannels

Description

List configuration channels associated to an activation key.

Parameters

- string sessionKey
- string key

Return Value

- array:

    - struct - Configuration Channel information

        - int "id"
        - int "orgId"
        - string "label"
        - string "name"
        - string "description"
        - struct "configChannelType"
        - struct - Configuration Channel Type information

            - int "id"
            - string "label"
            - string "name"
            - int "priority"

2.19 removeChildChannels

Description

Remove child channels from an activation key.

Parameters

- string sessionKey
- string key
- array:

  - string - childChannelLabel

Return Value

- int - 1 on success, exception thrown otherwise.

2.20 removeConfigChannels

Description

Remove configuration channels from the given activation keys.

Parameters

- string sessionKey
- array:

  - string - activationKey
- array:

  - string - configChannelLabel

Return Value

- int - 1 on success, exception thrown otherwise.

2.21 removeEntitlements

Description

Remove entitlements (by label) from an activation key. Currently only virtualization_host add-on entitlement is permitted.

Parameters

- string sessionKey
- string key
- array string - entitlement label

  - virtualization_host

Return Value

- int - 1 on success, exception thrown otherwise.

2.22   removePackageNames

Description

Remove package names from an activation key.

Deprecated - being replaced by removePackages(string sessionKey, string key, array[packages])

Available since: 10.2

Parameters

- string sessionKey
- string key
- array:

  - string - packageName

Return Value

- int - 1 on success, exception thrown otherwise.

2.23   removePackages

Description

Remove package names from an activation key.

Parameters

- string sessionKey
- string key
- array:

    - struct - packages

        - string "name" - Package name
        - string "arch" - Arch label - Optional

Return Value

- int - 1 on success, exception thrown otherwise.

2.24   removeServerGroups

Description

Remove server groups from an activation key.

Parameters

- string sessionKey
- string key
- array:

    - int - serverGroupId

Return Value

- int - 1 on success, exception thrown otherwise.

2.25   setConfigChannels

Description

Replace the existing set of configuration channels on the given activation keys. Channels are ranked by their order in the array.

Parameters

- string sessionKey
- array:

    - string - activationKey
- array:

    - string - configChannelLabel

Return Value

- int - 1 on success, exception thrown otherwise.

2.26 setDetails

Description

Update the details of an activation key.

Parameters

- string sessionKey
- string key
- struct - activation key

    - string "description" - optional
    - string "base_channel_label" - optional - to set default base channel set to empty string or 'none'
    - int "usage_limit" - optional
    - boolean "unlimited_usage_limit" - Set true for unlimited usage and to override usage_limit
    - boolean "universal_default" - optional
    - boolean "disabled" - optional
    - string "contact_method" - One of the following:
        - default
        - ssh-push
        - ssh-push-tunnel

Return Value

- int - 1 on success, exception thrown otherwise.

3 api

Methods providing information about the API.

3.1 getApiCallList

Description

   Lists all available api calls grouped by namespace

Parameters

   * string sessionKey

Return Value

   * struct - method_info

      * string "name" - method name
      * string "parameters" - method parameters
      * string "exceptions" - method exceptions
      * string "return" - method return type

3.2 getApiNamespaceCallList

Description

   Lists all available api calls for the specified namespace

Parameters

   * string sessionKey
   * string namespace

Return Value

   * struct - method_info

      * string "name" - method name
      * string "parameters" - method parameters

- string "exceptions" - method exceptions
- string "return" - method return type

3.3 getApiNamespaces

Description

Lists available API namespaces

Parameters

- string sessionKey

Return Value

- struct - namespace
    - string "namespace" - API namespace
    - string "handler" - API Handler

3.4 getVersion

Description

Returns the version of the API. Since Spacewalk 0.4 (Satellite 5.3) it is no more related to server version.

Parameters

- None

Return Value

- string

3.5 systemVersion

Description

Returns the server version.

Parameters

- None

Return Value

- string

systemVersion   SUSE Manager 3.1

4 audit

Methods to audit systems.

4.1 listImagesByPatchStatus

Description

List visible images with their patch status regarding a given CVE identifier. Please note that the query code relies on data that is pre-generated by the 'cve-server-channels' taskomatic job.

Parameters

- string sessionKey
- string cveIdentifier

Return Value

- array:

  - struct - cve_audit_image

    - int "image_id"
    - string "patch_status"
      - AFFECTED_PATCH_INAPPLICABLE - Affected, patch available in unassigned channel
      - AFFECTED_PATCH_APPLICABLE - Affected, patch available in assigned channel
      - NOT_AFFECTED - Not affected
      - PATCHED - Patched
    - array "string"

      - channel_labels - Labels of channels that contain an unapplied patch
    - array "string"

- errata_advisories - Advisories of erratas that patch the specified vulnerability

4.2 listImagesByPatchStatus

Description

List visible images with their patch status regarding a given CVE identifier. Filter the results by passing in a list of patch status labels. Please note that the query code relies on data that is pre-generated by the 'cve-server-channels' taskomatic job.

Parameters

- string sessionKey
- string cveIdentifier
- array:

  - string - patchStatusLabel
  - - AFFECTED_PATCH_INAPPLICABLE - Affected, patch available in unassigned channel
  - AFFECTED_PATCH_APPLICABLE - Affected, patch available in assigned channel
  - NOT_AFFECTED - Not affected
  - PATCHED - Patched

Return Value

- array:

  - struct - cve_audit_image

    - int "image_id"
    - string "patch_status"
    - - AFFECTED_PATCH_INAPPLICABLE - Affected, patch available in unassigned channel
    - AFFECTED_PATCH_APPLICABLE - Affected, patch available in assigned channel
    - NOT_AFFECTED - Not affected
    - PATCHED - Patched

- array "string"

  - channel_labels - Labels of channels that contain an unapplied patch
- array "string"

  - errata_advisories - Advisories of erratas that patch the specified vulnerability

4.3 listSystemsByPatchStatus

Description

List visible systems with their patch status regarding a given CVE identifier. Please note that the query code relies on data that is pre-generated by the 'cve-server-channels' taskomatic job.

Parameters

- string sessionKey
- string cveIdentifier

Return Value

- array:

  - struct - cve_audit_system

    - int "system_id"
    - string "patch_status"
      - AFFECTED_PATCH_INAPPLICABLE - Affected, patch available in unassigned channel
      - AFFECTED_PATCH_APPLICABLE - Affected, patch available in assigned channel
      - NOT_AFFECTED - Not affected
      - PATCHED - Patched
    - array "string"

      - channel_labels - Labels of channels that contain an unapplied patch
    - array "string"

- errata_advisories - Advisories of erratas that patch the specified vulnerability

4.4 listSystemsByPatchStatus

Description

List visible systems with their patch status regarding a given CVE identifier. Filter the results by passing in a list of patch status labels. Please note that the query code relies on data that is pre-generated by the 'cve-server-channels' taskomatic job.

Parameters

- string sessionKey
- string cveIdentifier
- array:

    - string - patchStatusLabel
    - AFFECTED_PATCH_INAPPLICABLE - Affected, patch available in unassigned channel
    - AFFECTED_PATCH_APPLICABLE - Affected, patch available in assigned channel
    - NOT_AFFECTED - Not affected
    - PATCHED - Patched

Return Value

- array:

    - struct - cve_audit_system

        - int "system_id"
        - string "patch_status"
        - AFFECTED_PATCH_INAPPLICABLE - Affected, patch available in unassigned channel
        - AFFECTED_PATCH_APPLICABLE - Affected, patch available in assigned channel
        - NOT_AFFECTED - Not affected
        - PATCHED - Patched

- array "string"

  - channel_labels - Labels of channels that contain an unapplied patch
- array "string"

  - errata_advisories - Advisories of erratas that patch the specified vulnerability

5 auth

This namespace provides methods to authenticate with the system's management server.

5.1 login

Description

Login using a username and password. Returns the session key used by most other API methods.

Parameters

- string username
- string password

Return Value

- string sessionKey

5.2 login

Description

Login using a username and password. Returns the session key used by other methods.

Parameters

- string username
- string password
- int duration - Length of session.

Return Value

- string sessionKey

5.3 logout

Description

Logout the user with the given session key.

Parameters

- string sessionKey

Return Value

- int - 1 on success, exception thrown otherwise.

6 channel

Provides method to get back a list of Software Channels.

6.1 listAllChannels

Description

List all software channels that the user's organization is entitled to.

Parameters

- string sessionKey

Return Value

- array:

    - struct - channel info

        - int "id"
        - string "label"
        - string "name"
        - string "provider_name"
        - int "packages"
        - int "systems"
        - string "arch_name"

6.2 listManageableChannels

Description

List all software channels that the user is entitled to manage.

Parameters

- string sessionKey

Return Value

- array:

  - struct - channel info

    - int "id"
    - string "label"
    - string "name"
    - string "provider_name"
    - int "packages"
    - int "systems"
    - string "arch_name"

6.3 listMyChannels

Description

List all software channels that belong to the user's organization.

Parameters

- string sessionKey

Return Value

- array:

  - struct - channel info

    - int "id"
    - string "label"
    - string "name"
    - string "provider_name"
    - int "packages"

- int "systems"
- string "arch_name"

6.4 listPopularChannels

Description

List the most popular software channels. Channels that have at least the number of systems subscribed as specified by the popularity count will be returned.

Parameters

- string sessionKey
- int popularityCount

Return Value

- array:

    - struct - channel info

        - int "id"
        - string "label"
        - string "name"
        - string "provider_name"
        - int "packages"
        - int "systems"
        - string "arch_name"

6.5 listRedHatChannels

Description

List all Red Hat software channels that the user's organization is entitled to.

Deprecated - being replaced by listVendorChannels(String sessionKey)

Parameters

- string sessionKey

Return Value

- array:

  - struct - channel info

    - int "id"
    - string "label"
    - string "name"
    - string "provider_name"
    - int "packages"
    - int "systems"
    - string "arch_name"

6.6 listRetiredChannels

Description

List all retired software channels. These are channels that the user's organization is entitled to, but are no longer supported because they have reached their 'end-of-life' date.

Parameters

- string sessionKey

Return Value

- array:

  - struct - channel info

    - int "id"
    - string "label"
    - string "name"
    - string "provider_name"
    - int "packages"

- int "systems"
- string "arch_name"

6.7 listSharedChannels

Description

List all software channels that may be shared by the user's organization.

Parameters

- string sessionKey

Return Value

- array:

    - struct - channel info

        - int "id"
        - string "label"
        - string "name"
        - string "provider_name"
        - int "packages"
        - int "systems"
        - string "arch_name"

6.8 listSoftwareChannels

Description

List all visible software channels.

Parameters

- string sessionKey

Return Value

- array:

    - struct - channel

- string "label"
- string "name"
- string "parent_label"
- string "end_of_life"
- string "arch"

6.9 listVendorChannels

Description

Lists all the vendor software channels that the user's organization is entitled to.

Parameters

- string sessionKey

Return Value

- array:

    - struct - channel info

        - int "id"
        - string "label"
        - string "name"
        - string "provider_name"
        - int "packages"
        - int "systems"
        - string "arch_name"

7 channel.access

Provides methods to retrieve and alter channel access restrictions.

7.1 disableUserRestrictions

Description

> Disable user restrictions for the given channel. If disabled, all users within the organization may subscribe to the channel.

Parameters

- string sessionKey
- string channelLabel - label of the channel

Return Value

- int - 1 on success, exception thrown otherwise.

7.2 enableUserRestrictions

Description

> Enable user restrictions for the given channel. If enabled, only selected users within the organization may subscribe to the channel.

Parameters

- string sessionKey
- string channelLabel - label of the channel

Return Value

- int - 1 on success, exception thrown otherwise.

7.3 getOrgSharing

Description

> Get organization sharing access control.

Parameters

- string sessionKey
- string channelLabel - label of the channel

Return Value

- string - The access value (one of the following: 'public', 'private', or 'protected'.

7.4 setOrgSharing

Description

Set organization sharing access control.

Parameters

- string sessionKey
- string channelLabel - label of the channel
- string access - Access (one of the following: 'public', 'private', or 'protected'

Return Value

- int - 1 on success, exception thrown otherwise.

8   channel.org

Provides methods to retrieve and alter organization trust relationships for a channel.

8.1   disableAccess

Description

Disable access to the channel for the given organization.

Parameters

- string sessionKey
- string channelLabel - label of the channel
- int orgId - id of org being removed access

Return Value

- int - 1 on success, exception thrown otherwise.

8.2   enableAccess

Description

Enable access to the channel for the given organization.

Parameters

- string sessionKey
- string channelLabel - label of the channel
- int orgId - id of org being granted access

Return Value

- int - 1 on success, exception thrown otherwise.

8.3 list

Description

List the organizations associated with the given channel that may be trusted.

Parameters

- string sessionKey
- string channelLabel - label of the channel

Return Value

- array:

    - struct - org

        - int "org_id"
        - string "org_name"
        - boolean "access_enabled"

9 channel.software

Provides methods to access and modify many aspects of a channel.

9.1 addPackages

Description

Adds a given list of packages to the given channel.

Parameters

- string sessionKey
- string channelLabel - target channel.
- array:

    - int - packageId - id of a package to add to the channel.

Return Value

- int - 1 on success, exception thrown otherwise.

9.2 addRepoFilter

Description

Adds a filter for a given repo.

Parameters

- string sessionKey
- string label - repository label
- struct - filter_map

    - string "filter" - string to filter on
    - string "flag" - + for include, - for exclude

Return Value

- int sort order for new filter

9.3 associateRepo

Description

Associates a repository with a channel

Parameters

- string sessionKey
- string channelLabel - channel label
- string repoLabel - repository label

Return Value

- struct - channel

    - int "id"
    - string "name"
    - string "label"
    - string "arch_name"
    - string "arch_label"
    - string "summary"
    - string "description"
    - string "checksum_label"
    - dateTime.iso8601 "last_modified"
    - string "maintainer_name"
    - string "maintainer_email"
    - string "maintainer_phone"
    - string "support_policy"
    - string "gpg_key_url"
    - string "gpg_key_id"
    - string "gpg_key_fp"
    - dateTime.iso8601 "yumrepo_last_sync" - (optional)
    - string "end_of_life"
    - string "parent_channel_label"

- string "clone_original"
- array:

  - struct - contentSources

    - int "id"
    - string "label"
    - string "sourceUrl"
    - string "type"

9.4 clearRepoFilters

Description

Removes the filters for a repo

Parameters

- string sessionKey
- string label - repository label

Return Value

- int - 1 on success, exception thrown otherwise.

9.5 clone

Description

Clone a channel. If arch_label is omitted, the arch label of the original channel will be used.
If parent_label is omitted, the clone will be a base channel.

Parameters

- string sessionKey
- string original_label
- struct - channel details

  - string "name"
  - string "label"

- string "summary"
- string "parent_label" - (optional)
- string "arch_label" - (optional)
- string "gpg_key_url" - (optional), gpg_url might be used as well
- string "gpg_key_id" - (optional), gpg_id might be used as well
- string "gpg_key_fp" - (optional), gpg_fingerprint might be used as well
- string "description" - (optional)
- string "checksum" - either sha1 or sha256
- boolean original_state

Return Value

- int the cloned channel ID

9.6 create

Description

Creates a software channel

Available since: 10.9

Parameters

- string sessionKey
- string label - label of the new channel
- string name - name of the new channel
- string summary - summary of the channel
- string archLabel - the label of the architecture the channel corresponds to, see channel.software.listArches API for complete listing
- string parentLabel - label of the parent of this channel, an empty string if it does not have one
- string checksumType - checksum type for this channel, used for yum repository metadata generation
  - sha1 - Offers widest compatibility with clients
  - sha256 - Offers highest security, but is compatible only with newer clients: Fedora 11 and newer, or Enterprise Linux 6 and newer.
- struct - gpgKey

- string "url" - GPG key URL
- string "id" - GPG key ID
- string "fingerprint" - GPG key Fingerprint

Return Value

- int - 1 if the creation operation succeeded, 0 otherwise

9.7 create

Description

Creates a software channel
Available since: 10.9

Parameters

- string sessionKey
- string label - label of the new channel
- string name - name of the new channel
- string summary - summary of the channel
- string archLabel - the label of the architecture the channel corresponds to, see channel.software.listArches API for complete listing
- string parentLabel - label of the parent of this channel, an empty string if it does not have one
- string checksumType - checksum type for this channel, used for yum repository metadata generation
  - sha1 - Offers widest compatibility with clients
    - sha256 - Offers highest security, but is compatible only with newer clients: Fedora 11 and newer, or Enterprise Linux 6 and newer.

Return Value

- int - 1 if the creation operation succeeded, 0 otherwise

9.8 create

Description

Creates a software channel

Parameters

- string sessionKey
- string label - label of the new channel
- string name - name of the new channel
- string summary - summary of the channel
- string archLabel - the label of the architecture the channel corresponds to, see channel.software.listArches API for complete listing
- string parentLabel - label of the parent of this channel, an empty string if it does not have one

Return Value

- int - 1 if the creation operation succeeded, 0 otherwise

9.9 createRepo

Description

Creates a repository

Parameters

- string sessionKey
- string label - repository label
- string type - repository type (yum, uln...)
- string url - repository url

Return Value

- struct - channel

    - int "id"
    - string "label"
    - string "sourceUrl"
    - string "type"
    - boolean "hasSignedMetadata"
    - array "sslContentSources" -

        - struct - contentsourcessl

            - string "sslCaDesc"
            - string "sslCertDesc"
            - string "sslKeyDesc"

9.10 createRepo

Description

Creates a repository

Parameters

- string sessionKey
- string label - repository label
- string type - repository type (yum, uln...)
- string url - repository url
- string sslCaCert - SSL CA cert description
- string sslCliCert - SSL Client cert description
- string sslCliKey - SSL Client key description

Return Value

- struct - channel

    - int "id"
    - string "label"

- string "sourceUrl"
- string "type"
- boolean "hasSignedMetadata"
- array "sslContentSources" -

    - struct - contentsourcessl

        - string "sslCaDesc"
        - string "sslCertDesc"
        - string "sslKeyDesc"

9.11 createRepo

Description

Creates a repository

Parameters

- string sessionKey
- string label - repository label
- string type - repository type (only YUM is supported)
- string url - repository url
- string sslCaCert - SSL CA cert description, or an empty string
- string sslCliCert - SSL Client cert description, or an empty string
- string sslCliKey - SSL Client key description, or an empty string
- boolean hasSignedMetadata - true if the repository has signed metadata, false otherwise

Return Value

- struct - channel

    - int "id"
    - string "label"
    - string "sourceUrl"
    - string "type"
    - boolean "hasSignedMetadata"
    - array "sslContentSources" -

- struct - contentsourcessl
    - string "sslCaDesc"
    - string "sslCertDesc"
    - string "sslKeyDesc"

9.12 delete

Description

Deletes a custom software channel

Parameters

- string sessionKey
- string channelLabel - channel to delete

Return Value

- int - 1 on success, exception thrown otherwise.

9.13 disassociateRepo

Description

Disassociates a repository from a channel

Parameters

- string sessionKey
- string channelLabel - channel label
- string repoLabel - repository label

Return Value

- struct - channel
    - int "id"
    - string "name"

- string "label"
- string "arch_name"
- string "arch_label"
- string "summary"
- string "description"
- string "checksum_label"
- dateTime.iso8601 "last_modified"
- string "maintainer_name"
- string "maintainer_email"
- string "maintainer_phone"
- string "support_policy"
- string "gpg_key_url"
- string "gpg_key_id"
- string "gpg_key_fp"
- dateTime.iso8601 "yumrepo_last_sync" - (optional)
- string "end_of_life"
- string "parent_channel_label"
- string "clone_original"
- array:

  - struct - contentSources

    - int "id"
    - string "label"
    - string "sourceUrl"
    - string "type"

9.14 getChannelLastBuildById

Description

Returns the last build date of the repomd.xml file for the given channel as a localised string.

Parameters

- string sessionKey
- int id - id of channel wanted

Return Value

* the last build date of the repomd.xml file as a localised string

9.15 getDetails

Description

Returns details of the given channel as a map

Parameters

* string sessionKey
* string channelLabel - channel to query

Return Value

* struct - channel

    * int "id"
    * string "name"
    * string "label"
    * string "arch_name"
    * string "arch_label"
    * string "summary"
    * string "description"
    * string "checksum_label"
    * dateTime.iso8601 "last_modified"
    * string "maintainer_name"
    * string "maintainer_email"
    * string "maintainer_phone"
    * string "support_policy"
    * string "gpg_key_url"
    * string "gpg_key_id"
    * string "gpg_key_fp"
    * dateTime.iso8601 "yumrepo_last_sync" - (optional)
    * string "end_of_life"
    * string "parent_channel_label"

- string "clone_original"
- array:

  - struct - contentSources

    - int "id"
    - string "label"
    - string "sourceUrl"
    - string "type"

9.16 getDetails

Description

Returns details of the given channel as a map

Parameters

- string sessionKey
- int id - channel to query

Return Value

- struct - channel

  - int "id"
  - string "name"
  - string "label"
  - string "arch_name"
  - string "arch_label"
  - string "summary"
  - string "description"
  - string "checksum_label"
  - dateTime.iso8601 "last_modified"
  - string "maintainer_name"
  - string "maintainer_email"
  - string "maintainer_phone"
  - string "support_policy"
  - string "gpg_key_url"

- string "gpg_key_id"
- string "gpg_key_fp"
- dateTime.iso8601 "yumrepo_last_sync" - (optional)
- string "end_of_life"
- string "parent_channel_label"
- string "clone_original"
- array:

  - struct - contentSources

    - int "id"
    - string "label"
    - string "sourceUrl"
    - string "type"

9.17 getRepoDetails

Description

Returns details of the given repository

Parameters

- string sessionKey
- string repoLabel - repo to query

Return Value

- struct - channel

  - int "id"
  - string "label"
  - string "sourceUrl"
  - string "type"
  - boolean "hasSignedMetadata"
  - array "sslContentSources" -

    - struct - contentsourcessl

- string "sslCaDesc"
- string "sslCertDesc"
- string "sslKeyDesc"

9.18 getRepoDetails

Description

Returns details of the given repository

Parameters

- string sessionKey
- int id - repository id

Return Value

- struct - channel

    - int "id"
    - string "label"
    - string "sourceUrl"
    - string "type"
    - boolean "hasSignedMetadata"
    - array "sslContentSources" -

        - struct - contentsourcessl

            - string "sslCaDesc"
            - string "sslCertDesc"
            - string "sslKeyDesc"

9.19 getRepoSyncCronExpression

Description

Returns repo synchronization cron expression

Parameters

- string sessionKey
- string channelLabel - channel label

Return Value

- string quartz expression

9.20 isGloballySubscribable

Description

Returns whether the channel is subscribable by any user in the organization

Parameters

- string sessionKey
- string channelLabel - channel to query

Return Value

- int - 1 if true, 0 otherwise

9.21 isUserManageable

Description

Returns whether the channel may be managed by the given user.

Parameters

- string sessionKey
- string channelLabel - label of the channel
- string login - login of the target user

Return Value

- int - 1 if manageable, 0 if not

9.22 isUserSubscribable

Description

Returns whether the channel may be subscribed to by the given user.

Parameters

- string sessionKey
- string channelLabel - label of the channel
- string login - login of the target user

Return Value

- int - 1 if subscribable, 0 if not

9.23 listAllPackages

Description

Lists all packages in the channel, regardless of package version, between the given dates.

Parameters

- string sessionKey
- string channelLabel - channel to query
- dateTime.iso8601 startDate
- dateTime.iso8601 endDate

Return Value

- array:

  - struct - package

    - string "name"
    - string "version"

- string "release"
- string "epoch"
- string "checksum"
- string "checksum_type"
- int "id"
- string "arch_label"
- string "last_modified_date"
- string "last_modified" - (Deprecated)

9.24 listAllPackages

Description

Lists all packages in the channel, regardless of version whose last modified date is greater than given date.

Parameters

- string sessionKey
- string channelLabel - channel to query
- dateTime.iso8601 startDate

Return Value

- array:

  - struct - package

    - string "name"
    - string "version"
    - string "release"
    - string "epoch"
    - string "checksum"
    - string "checksum_type"
    - int "id"
    - string "arch_label"

- string "last_modified_date"
- string "last_modified" - (Deprecated)

9.25   listAllPackages

Description

Lists all packages in the channel, regardless of the package version

Parameters

- string sessionKey
- string channelLabel - channel to query

Return Value

- array:

  - struct - package

    - string "name"
    - string "version"
    - string "release"
    - string "epoch"
    - string "checksum"
    - string "checksum_type"
    - int "id"
    - string "arch_label"
    - string "last_modified_date"
    - string "last_modified" - (Deprecated)

9.26   listAllPackages

Description

Lists all packages in the channel, regardless of package version, between the given dates. Example Date: '2008-08-20 08:00:00'

Deprecated - being replaced by listAllPackages(string sessionKey, string channelLabel, dateTime.iso8601 startDate, dateTime.iso8601 endDate)

Parameters

- string sessionKey
- string channelLabel - channel to query
- string startDate
- string endDate

Return Value

- array:

    - struct - package

        - string "name"
        - string "version"
        - string "release"
        - string "epoch"
        - string "checksum"
        - string "checksum_type"
        - int "id"
        - string "arch_label"
        - string "last_modified_date"
        - string "last_modified" - (Deprecated)

9.27 listAllPackages

Description

Lists all packages in the channel, regardless of version whose last modified date is greater than given date. Example Date: '2008-08-20 08:00:00'

Deprecated - being replaced by listAllPackages(string sessionKey, string channelLabel, dateTime.iso8601 startDate)

Parameters

- string sessionKey
- string channelLabel - channel to query
- string startDate

Return Value

- array:

  - struct - package

    - string "name"
    - string "version"
    - string "release"
    - string "epoch"
    - string "checksum"
    - string "checksum_type"
    - int "id"
    - string "arch_label"
    - string "last_modified_date"
    - string "last_modified" - (Deprecated)

9.28 listAllPackagesByDate

Description

Lists all packages in the channel, regardless of the package version, between the given dates. Example Date: '2008-08-20 08:00:00'

Deprecated - being replaced by listAllPackages(string sessionKey, string channelLabel, dateTime.iso8601 startDate, dateTime.iso8601 endDate)

Parameters

- string sessionKey
- string channelLabel - channel to query
- string startDate
- string endDate

Return Value

- array:

  - struct - package

- string "name"
- string "version"
- string "release"
- string "epoch"
- string "id"
- string "arch_label"
- string "last_modified"

9.29 listAllPackagesByDate

Description

Lists all packages in the channel, regardless of the package version, whose last modified date is greater than given date. Example Date: '2008-08-20 08:00:00'

Deprecated - being replaced by listAllPackages(string sessionKey, string channelLabel, dateTime.iso8601 startDate)

Parameters

- string sessionKey
- string channelLabel - channel to query
- string startDate

Return Value

- array:

    - struct - package

        - string "name"
        - string "version"
        - string "release"
        - string "epoch"
        - string "id"

- string "arch_label"
- string "last_modified"

9.30 listAllPackagesByDate

Description

Lists all packages in the channel, regardless of the package version

Deprecated - being replaced by listAllPackages(string sessionKey, string channelLabel)

Parameters

- string sessionKey
- string channelLabel - channel to query

Return Value

- array:

    - struct - package

        - string "name"
        - string "version"
        - string "release"
        - string "epoch"
        - string "id"
        - string "arch_label"
        - string "last_modified"

9.31 listArches

Description

Lists the potential software channel architectures that can be created

Parameters

- string sessionKey

Return Value

- array:

  - struct - channel arch

    - string "name"
    - string "label"

9.32 listChannelRepos

Description

Lists associated repos with the given channel

Parameters

- string sessionKey
- string channelLabel - channel label

Return Value

- array:

  - struct - channel

    - int "id"
    - string "label"
    - string "sourceUrl"
    - string "type"
    - boolean "hasSignedMetadata"
    - array "sslContentSources" -

      - struct - contentsourcessl

- string "sslCaDesc"
- string "sslCertDesc"
- string "sslKeyDesc"

9.33 listChildren

Description

> List the children of a channel

Parameters

- string sessionKey
- string channelLabel - the label of the channel

Return Value

- array:

  - struct - channel

    - int "id"
    - string "name"
    - string "label"
    - string "arch_name"
    - string "arch_label"
    - string "summary"
    - string "description"
    - string "checksum_label"
    - dateTime.iso8601 "last_modified"
    - string "maintainer_name"
    - string "maintainer_email"
    - string "maintainer_phone"
    - string "support_policy"
    - string "gpg_key_url"
    - string "gpg_key_id"
    - string "gpg_key_fp"
    - dateTime.iso8601 "yumrepo_last_sync" - (optional)

- string "end_of_life"
- string "parent_channel_label"
- string "clone_original"
- array:

    - struct - contentSources

        - int "id"
        - string "label"
        - string "sourceUrl"
        - string "type"

9.34 listErrata

Description

List the errata applicable to a channel after given startDate

Parameters

- string sessionKey
- string channelLabel - channel to query
- dateTime.iso8601 startDate

Return Value

- array:

    - struct - errata

        - int "id" - Errata ID.
        - string "date" - Date erratum was created.
        - string "update_date" - Date erratum was updated.
        - string "advisory_synopsis" - Summary of the erratum.

- string "advisory_type" - Type label such as Security, Bug Fix
- string "advisory_name" - Name such as RHSA, etc

9.35 listErrata

Description

List the errata applicable to a channel between startDate and endDate.

Parameters

- string sessionKey
- string channelLabel - channel to query
- dateTime.iso8601 startDate
- dateTime.iso8601 endDate

Return Value

- array:

  - struct - errata

    - int "id" - Errata ID.
    - string "date" - Date erratum was created.
    - string "update_date" - Date erratum was updated.
    - string "advisory_synopsis" - Summary of the erratum.
    - string "advisory_type" - Type label such as Security, Bug Fix
    - string "advisory_name" - Name such as RHSA, etc

9.36 listErrata

Description

List the errata applicable to a channel between startDate and endDate.

Parameters

- string sessionKey
- string channelLabel - channel to query
- dateTime.iso8601 startDate

- dateTime.iso8601 endDate
- boolean lastModified - select by last modified or not

Return Value

- array:

    - struct - errata

        - int "id" - Errata ID.
        - string "date" - Date erratum was created.
        - string "update_date" - Date erratum was updated.
        - string "advisory_synopsis" - Summary of the erratum.
        - string "advisory_type" - Type label such as Security, Bug Fix
        - string "advisory_name" - Name such as RHSA, etc

9.37 listErrata

Description

List the errata applicable to a channel

Parameters

- string sessionKey
- string channelLabel - channel to query

Return Value

- array:

    - struct - errata

        - int "id" - Errata Id
        - string "advisory_synopsis" - Summary of the erratum.
        - string "advisory_type" - Type label such as Security, Bug Fix
        - string "advisory_name" - Name such as RHSA, etc
        - string "advisory" - name of the advisory (Deprecated)
        - string "issue_date" - date format follows YYYY-MM-DD HH24:MI:SS (Deprecated)

- string "update_date" - date format follows YYYY-MM-DD HH24:MI:SS (Deprecated)
- string "synopsis (Deprecated)"
- string "last_modified_date" - date format follows YYYY-MM-DD HH24:MI:SS (Deprecated)

9.38 listErrata

Description

List the errata applicable to a channel after given startDate

Deprecated - being replaced by listErrata(string sessionKey, string channelLabel, date-Time.iso8601 startDate)

Parameters

- string sessionKey
- string channelLabel - channel to query
- string startDate

Return Value

- array:

    - struct - errata

        - string "advisory" - name of the advisory
        - string "issue_date" - date format follows YYYY-MM-DD HH24:MI:SS
        - string "update_date" - date format follows YYYY-MM-DD HH24:MI:SS
        - string "synopsis"
        - string "advisory_type"
        - string "last_modified_date" - date format follows YYYY-MM-DD HH24:MI:SS

9.39 listErrata

Description

List the errata applicable to a channel between startDate and endDate.

Deprecated - being replaced by listErrata(string sessionKey, string channelLabel, date-Time.iso8601 startDate, dateTime.iso8601)

Parameters

- string sessionKey
- string channelLabel - channel to query
- string startDate
- string endDate

Return Value

- array:

  - struct - errata

    - string "advisory" - name of the advisory
    - string "issue_date" - date format follows YYYY-MM-DD HH24:MI:SS
    - string "update_date" - date format follows YYYY-MM-DD HH24:MI:SS
    - string "synopsis"
    - string "advisory_type"
    - string "last_modified_date" - date format follows YYYY-MM-DD HH24:MI:SS

9.40 listErrataByType

Description

List the errata of a specific type that are applicable to a channel

Parameters

- string sessionKey
- string channelLabel - channel to query
- string advisoryType - type of advisory (one of of the following: 'Security Advisory', 'Product Enhancement Advisory', 'Bug Fix Advisory'

Return Value

- array:

  - struct - errata

    - string "advisory" - name of the advisory
    - string "issue_date" - date format follows YYYY-MM-DD HH24:MI:SS
    - string "update_date" - date format follows YYYY-MM-DD HH24:MI:SS
    - string "synopsis"
    - string "advisory_type"
    - string "last_modified_date" - date format follows YYYY-MM-DD HH24:MI:SS

9.41 listErrataNeedingSync

Description

If you have satellite-synced a new channel then Red Hat Errata will have been updated with the packages that are in the newly synced channel. A cloned erratum will not have been automatically updated however. If you cloned a channel that includes those cloned errata and should include the new packages, they will not be included when they should. This method lists the errata that will be updated if you run the syncErrata method.

Parameters

- string sessionKey
- string channelLabel - channel to update

Return Value

- array:

  - struct - errata

    - int "id" - Errata ID.
    - string "date" - Date erratum was created.
    - string "update_date" - Date erratum was updated.
    - string "advisory_synopsis" - Summary of the erratum.

- string "advisory_type" - Type label such as Security, Bug Fix
- string "advisory_name" - Name such as RHSA, etc

9.42 listLatestPackages

Description

Lists the packages with the latest version (including release and epoch) for the given channel

Parameters

- string sessionKey
- string channelLabel - channel to query

Return Value

- array:

  - struct - package

    - string "name"
    - string "version"
    - string "release"
    - string "epoch"
    - int "id"
    - string "arch_label"

9.43 listPackagesWithoutChannel

Description

Lists all packages that are not associated with a channel. Typically these are custom packages.

Parameters

- string sessionKey

Return Value

- array:

    - struct - package

        - string "name"
        - string "version"
        - string "release"
        - string "epoch"
        - int "id"
        - string "arch_label"
        - string "path" - The path on that file system that the package resides
        - string "provider" - The provider of the package, determined by the gpg key it was signed with.
        - dateTime.iso8601 "last_modified"

9.44 listRepoFilters

Description

Lists the filters for a repo

Parameters

- string sessionKey
- string label - repository label

Return Value

- array:

    - struct - filter

listRepoFilters   SUSE Manager 3.1

- int "sortOrder"
- string "filter"
- string "flag"

9.45 listSubscribedSystems

Description

Returns list of subscribed systems for the given channel label

Parameters

- string sessionKey
- string channelLabel - channel to query

Return Value

- array:

  - struct - system

    - int "id"
    - string "name"

9.46 listSystemChannels

Description

Returns a list of channels that a system is subscribed to for the given system id

Parameters

- string sessionKey
- int serverId

Return Value

- array:

  - struct - channel

- string "id"
- string "label"
- string "name"

9.47 listUserRepos

Description

Returns a list of ContentSource (repos) that the user can see

Parameters

- string sessionKey

Return Value

- array:

    - struct - map

        - long "id" - ID of the repo
        - string "label" - label of the repo
        - string "sourceUrl" - URL of the repo

9.48 mergeErrata

Description

Merges all errata from one channel into another

Parameters

- string sessionKey
- string mergeFromLabel - the label of the channel to pull errata from
- string mergeToLabel - the label to push the errata into

Return Value

- array:

    - struct - errata

- int "id" - Errata Id
- string "date" - Date erratum was created.
- string "advisory_type" - Type of the advisory.
- string "advisory_name" - Name of the advisory.
- string "advisory_synopsis" - Summary of the erratum.

9.49 mergeErrata

Description

Merges all errata from one channel into another based upon a given start/end date.

Parameters

- string sessionKey
- string mergeFromLabel - the label of the channel to pull errata from
- string mergeToLabel - the label to push the errata into
- string startDate
- string endDate

Return Value

- array:

    - struct - errata

        - int "id" - Errata Id
        - string "date" - Date erratum was created.
        - string "advisory_type" - Type of the advisory.
        - string "advisory_name" - Name of the advisory.
        - string "advisory_synopsis" - Summary of the erratum.

9.50 mergeErrata

Description

Merges a list of errata from one channel into another

Parameters

- string sessionKey
- string mergeFromLabel - the label of the channel to pull errata from
- string mergeToLabel - the label to push the errata into
- array:

  - string - advisory - The advisory name of the errata to merge

Return Value

- array:

  - struct - errata

    - int "id" - Errata Id
    - string "date" - Date erratum was created.
    - string "advisory_type" - Type of the advisory.
    - string "advisory_name" - Name of the advisory.
    - string "advisory_synopsis" - Summary of the erratum.

9.51 mergePackages

Description

Merges all packages from one channel into another

Parameters

- string sessionKey
- string mergeFromLabel - the label of the channel to pull packages from
- string mergeToLabel - the label to push the packages into

Return Value

- array:

  - struct - package

    - string "name"
    - string "version"

- string "release"
- string "epoch"
- int "id"
- string "arch_label"
- string "path" - The path on that file system that the package resides
- string "provider" - The provider of the package, determined by the gpg key it was signed with.
- dateTime.iso8601 "last_modified"

9.52 regenerateNeededCache

Description

Completely clear and regenerate the needed Errata and Package cache for all systems subscribed to the specified channel. This should be used only if you believe your cache is incorrect for all the systems in a given channel. This will schedule an asynchronous action to actually do the processing.

Parameters

- string sessionKey
- string channelLabel - the label of the channel

Return Value

- int - 1 on success, exception thrown otherwise.

9.53 regenerateNeededCache

Description

Completely clear and regenerate the needed Errata and Package cache for all systems subscribed. You must be a Satellite Admin to perform this action. This will schedule an asynchronous action to actually do the processing.

Parameters

- string sessionKey

Return Value

- int - 1 on success, exception thrown otherwise.

9.54   regenerateYumCache

Description

Regenerate yum cache for the specified channel.

Parameters

- string sessionKey
- string channelLabel - the label of the channel

Return Value

- int - 1 on success, exception thrown otherwise.

9.55   removeErrata

Description

Removes a given list of errata from the given channel.

Parameters

- string sessionKey
- string channelLabel - target channel.
- array:

    - string - advisoryName - name of an erratum to remove
- boolean removePackages - True to remove packages from the channel

Return Value

- int - 1 on success, exception thrown otherwise.

9.56   removePackages

Description

Removes a given list of packages from the given channel.

Parameters

- string sessionKey
- string channelLabel - target channel.
- array:

    - int - packageId - id of a package to remove from the channel.

Return Value

- int - 1 on success, exception thrown otherwise.

9.57   removeRepo

Description

Removes a repository

Parameters

- string sessionKey
- long id - ID of repo to be removed

Return Value

- int - 1 on success, exception thrown otherwise.

9.58   removeRepo

Description

Removes a repository

Parameters

- string sessionKey
- string label - label of repo to be removed

Return Value

- int - 1 on success, exception thrown otherwise.

9.59 removeRepoFilter

Description

Removes a filter for a given repo.

Parameters

- string sessionKey
- string label - repository label
- struct - filter_map

    - string "filter" - string to filter on
    - string "flag" - + for include, - for exclude

Return Value

- int - 1 on success, exception thrown otherwise.

9.60 setContactDetails

Description

Set contact/support information for given channel.

Parameters

- string sessionKey
- string channelLabel - label of the channel
- string maintainerName - name of the channel maintainer
- string maintainerEmail - email of the channel maintainer

- string maintainerPhone - phone number of the channel maintainer
- string supportPolicy - channel support policy

Return Value

- int - 1 on success, exception thrown otherwise.

9.61 setDetails

Description

Allows to modify channel attributes

Parameters

- string sessionKey
- int channelId - channel id
- struct - channel_map

    - string "checksum_label" - new channel repository checksum label (optional)
    - string "name" - new channel name (optional)
    - string "summary" - new channel summary (optional)
    - string "description" - new channel description (optional)
    - string "maintainer_name" - new channel maintainer name (optional)
    - string "maintainer_email" - new channel email address (optional)
    - string "maintainer_phone" - new channel phone number (optional)
    - string "gpg_key_url" - new channel gpg key url (optional)
    - string "gpg_key_id" - new channel gpg key id (optional)
    - string "gpg_key_fp" - new channel gpg key fingerprint (optional)

Return Value

- int - 1 on success, exception thrown otherwise.

9.62 setGloballySubscribable

Description

Set globally subscribable attribute for given channel.

Parameters

- string sessionKey
- string channelLabel - label of the channel
- boolean subscribable - true if the channel is to be globally subscribable. False otherwise.

Return Value

- int - 1 on success, exception thrown otherwise.

9.63 setRepoFilters

Description

Replaces the existing set of filters for a given repo. Filters are ranked by their order in the array.

Parameters

- string sessionKey
- string label - repository label
- array:

  - struct - filter_map

    - string "filter" - string to filter on
    - string "flag" - + for include, - for exclude

Return Value

- int - 1 on success, exception thrown otherwise.

9.64 setSystemChannels

Description

Change a systems subscribed channels to the list of channels passed in.

Deprecated - being replaced by system.setBaseChannel(string sessionKey, int serverId, string channelLabel) and system.setChildChannels(string sessionKey, int serverId, array[string channelLabel])

Parameters

- string sessionKey
- int serverId
- array:

    - string - channelLabel - labels of the channels to subscribe the system to.

Return Value

- int - 1 on success, exception thrown otherwise.

9.65 setUserManageable

Description

Set the manageable flag for a given channel and user. If value is set to 'true', this method will give the user manage permissions to the channel. Otherwise, that privilege is revoked.

Parameters

- string sessionKey
- string channelLabel - label of the channel
- string login - login of the target user
- boolean value - value of the flag to set

Return Value

- int - 1 on success, exception thrown otherwise.

9.66 setUserSubscribable

Description

Set the subscribable flag for a given channel and user. If value is set to 'true', this method will give the user subscribe permissions to the channel. Otherwise, that privilege is revoked.

Parameters

- string sessionKey
- string channelLabel - label of the channel
- string login - login of the target user
- boolean value - value of the flag to set

Return Value

- int - 1 on success, exception thrown otherwise.

9.67 subscribeSystem

Description

Subscribes a system to a list of channels. If a base channel is included, that is set before setting child channels. When setting child channels the current child channel subscriptions are cleared. To fully unsubscribe the system from all channels, simply provide an empty list of channel labels.

Deprecated - being replaced by system.setBaseChannel(string sessionKey, int serverId, string channelLabel) and system.setChildChannels(string sessionKey, int serverId, array[string channelLabel])

Parameters

- string sessionKey
- int serverId
- array:

    - string - label - channel label to subscribe the system to.

Return Value

- int - 1 on success, exception thrown otherwise.

9.68 syncErrata

Description

If you have satellite-synced a new channel then Red Hat Errata will have been updated with the packages that are in the newly synced channel. A cloned erratum will not have been automatically updated however. If you cloned a channel that includes those cloned errata and should include the new packages, they will not be included when they should. This method updates all the errata in the given cloned channel with packages that have recently been added, and ensures that all the packages you expect are in the channel.

Parameters

- string sessionKey
- string channelLabel - channel to update

Return Value

- int - 1 on success, exception thrown otherwise.

9.69 syncRepo

Description

Trigger immediate repo synchronization

Parameters

- string sessionKey
- array:

    - string - channelLabels

Return Value

- int - 1 on success, exception thrown otherwise.

9.70 syncRepo

Description

   Trigger immediate repo synchronization

Parameters

- string sessionKey
- string channelLabel - channel label

Return Value

- int - 1 on success, exception thrown otherwise.

9.71 syncRepo

Description

   Trigger immediate repo synchronization

Parameters

- string sessionKey
- string channelLabel - channel label
- struct - params_map

    - Boolean "sync-kickstart" - Create kickstartable tree - Optional
    - Boolean "no-errata" - Do not sync errata - Optional
    - Boolean "fail" - Terminate upon any error - Optional

Return Value

- int - 1 on success, exception thrown otherwise.

9.72 syncRepo

Description

Schedule periodic repo synchronization

Parameters

- string sessionKey
- string channelLabel - channel label
- string cron expression - if empty all periodic schedules will be disabled

Return Value

- int - 1 on success, exception thrown otherwise.

9.73 syncRepo

Description

Schedule periodic repo synchronization

Parameters

- string sessionKey
- string channelLabel - channel label
- string cron expression - if empty all periodic schedules will be disabled
- struct - params_map

  - Boolean "sync-kickstart" - Create kickstartable tree - Optional
  - Boolean "no-errata" - Do not sync errata - Optional
  - Boolean "fail" - Terminate upon any error - Optional

Return Value

- int - 1 on success, exception thrown otherwise.

9.74 updateRepo

Description

Updates a ContentSource (repo)

Parameters

- string sessionKey
- int id - repository id
- string label - new repository label
- string url - new repository URL

Return Value

- struct - channel

    - int "id"
    - string "label"
    - string "sourceUrl"
    - string "type"
    - boolean "hasSignedMetadata"
    - array "sslContentSources" -

        - struct - contentsourcessl

            - string "sslCaDesc"
            - string "sslCertDesc"
            - string "sslKeyDesc"

9.75 updateRepoLabel

Description

Updates repository label

Parameters

- string sessionKey
- int id - repository id
- string label - new repository label

Return Value

- struct - channel

    - int "id"
    - string "label"
    - string "sourceUrl"
    - string "type"
    - boolean "hasSignedMetadata"
    - array "sslContentSources" -

        - struct - contentsourcessl

            - string "sslCaDesc"
            - string "sslCertDesc"
            - string "sslKeyDesc"

9.76 updateRepoLabel

Description

Updates repository label

Parameters

- string sessionKey
- string label - repository label
- string newLabel - new repository label

Return Value

- struct - channel

    - int "id"
    - string "label"

- string "sourceUrl"
- string "type"
- boolean "hasSignedMetadata"
- array "sslContentSources" -

    - struct - contentsourcessl

        - string "sslCaDesc"
        - string "sslCertDesc"
        - string "sslKeyDesc"

9.77 updateRepoSsl

Description

Updates repository SSL certificates

Parameters

- string sessionKey
- int id - repository id
- string sslCaCert - SSL CA cert description
- string sslCliCert - SSL Client cert description
- string sslCliKey - SSL Client key description

Return Value

- struct - channel

    - int "id"
    - string "label"
    - string "sourceUrl"
    - string "type"
    - boolean "hasSignedMetadata"
    - array "sslContentSources" -

        - struct - contentsourcessl

- string "sslCaDesc"
- string "sslCertDesc"
- string "sslKeyDesc"

9.78 `updateRepoSsl`

Description

Updates repository SSL certificates

Parameters

- string sessionKey
- string label - repository label
- string sslCaCert - SSL CA cert description
- string sslCliCert - SSL Client cert description
- string sslCliKey - SSL Client key description

Return Value

- struct - channel

  - int "id"
  - string "label"
  - string "sourceUrl"
  - string "type"
  - boolean "hasSignedMetadata"
  - array "sslContentSources" -

    - struct - contentsourcessl

- string "sslCaDesc"
- string "sslCertDesc"
- string "sslKeyDesc"

9.79 updateRepoUrl

Description

> Updates repository source URL

Parameters

- string sessionKey
- int id - repository id
- string url - new repository url

Return Value

- struct - channel

    - int "id"
    - string "label"
    - string "sourceUrl"
    - string "type"
    - boolean "hasSignedMetadata"
    - array "sslContentSources" -

        - struct - contentsourcessl

            - string "sslCaDesc"
            - string "sslCertDesc"
            - string "sslKeyDesc"

9.80 updateRepoUrl

Description

> Updates repository source URL

Parameters

- string sessionKey
- string label - repository label
- string url - new repository url

Return Value

- struct - channel

    - int "id"
    - string "label"
    - string "sourceUrl"
    - string "type"
    - boolean "hasSignedMetadata"
    - array "sslContentSources" -

        - struct - contentsourcessl

            - string "sslCaDesc"
            - string "sslCertDesc"
            - string "sslKeyDesc"

10 configchannel

Provides methods to access and modify many aspects of configuration channels.

10.1 channelExists

Description

> Check for the existence of the config channel provided.

Parameters

- string sessionKey
- string channelLabel - Channel to check for.

Return Value

- 1 if exists, 0 otherwise.

10.2 create

Description

> Create a new global config channel. Caller must be at least a config admin or an organization admin.

Parameters

- string sessionKey
- string channelLabel
- string channelName
- string channelDescription

Return Value

- struct - Configuration Channel information

  - int "id"
  - int "orgId"
  - string "label"
  - string "name"

- string "description"
- struct "configChannelType"
- struct - Configuration Channel Type information

    - int "id"
    - string "label"
    - string "name"
    - int "priority"

10.3 createOrUpdatePath

Description

Create a new file or directory with the given path, or update an existing path.
Available since: 10.2

Parameters

- string sessionKey
- string configChannelLabel
- string path
- boolean isDir - True if the path is a directory, False if it is a file.
- struct - path info

    - string "contents" - Contents of the file (text or base64 encoded if binary). (only for non-directories)
    - boolean "contents_enc64" - Identifies base64 encoded content (default: disabled, only for non-directories)
    - string "owner" - Owner of the file/directory.
    - string "group" - Group name of the file/directory.
    - string "permissions" - Octal file/directory permissions (eg: 644)
    - string "selinux_ctx" - SELinux Security context (optional)
    - string "macro-start-delimiter" - Config file macro start delimiter. Use null or empty string to accept the default. (only for non-directories)
    - string "macro-end-delimiter" - Config file macro end delimiter. Use null or empty string to accept the default. (only for non-directories)

- int "revision" - next revision number, auto increment for null
- boolean "binary" - mark the binary content, if True, base64 encoded content is expected (only for non-directories)

Return Value

- struct - Configuration Revision information

  - string "type"
    - file
    - directory
    - symlink
  - string "path" - File Path
  - string "target_path" - Symbolic link Target File Path. Present for Symbolic links only.
  - string "channel" - Channel Name
  - string "contents" - File contents (base64 encoded according to the contents_enc64 attribute)
  - boolean "contents_enc64" - Identifies base64 encoded content
  - int "revision" - File Revision
  - dateTime.iso8601 "creation" - Creation Date
  - dateTime.iso8601 "modified" - Last Modified Date
  - string "owner" - File Owner. Present for files or directories only.
  - string "group" - File Group. Present for files or directories only.
  - int "permissions" - File Permissions (Deprecated). Present for files or directories only.
  - string "permissions_mode" - File Permissions. Present for files or directories only.
  - string "selinux_ctx" - SELinux Context (optional).
  - boolean "binary" - true/false , Present for files only.
  - string "sha256" - File's sha256 signature. Present for files only.

- string "macro-start-delimiter" - Macro start delimiter for a config file. Present for text files only.
- string "macro-end-delimiter" - Macro end delimiter for a config file. Present for text files only.

10.4 createOrUpdateSymlink

Description

Create a new symbolic link with the given path, or update an existing path.

Available since: 10.2

Parameters

- string sessionKey
- string configChannelLabel
- string path
- struct - path info

  - string "target_path" - The target path for the symbolic link
  - string "selinux_ctx" - SELinux Security context (optional)
  - int "revision" - next revision number, skip this field for automatic revision number assignment

Return Value

- struct - Configuration Revision information

  - string "type"
    - file
    - directory
    - symlink
  - string "path" - File Path
  - string "target_path" - Symbolic link Target File Path. Present for Symbolic links only.
  - string "channel" - Channel Name
  - string "contents" - File contents (base64 encoded according to the contents_enc64 attribute)
  - boolean "contents_enc64" - Identifies base64 encoded content

- int "revision" - File Revision
- dateTime.iso8601 "creation" - Creation Date
- dateTime.iso8601 "modified" - Last Modified Date
- string "owner" - File Owner. Present for files or directories only.
- string "group" - File Group. Present for files or directories only.
- int "permissions" - File Permissions (Deprecated). Present for files or directories only.
- string "permissions_mode" - File Permissions. Present for files or directories only.
- string "selinux_ctx" - SELinux Context (optional).
- boolean "binary" - true/false , Present for files only.
- string "sha256" - File's sha256 signature. Present for files only.
- string "macro-start-delimiter" - Macro start delimiter for a config file. Present for text files only.
- string "macro-end-delimiter" - Macro end delimiter for a config file. Present for text files only.

10.5 deleteChannels

Description

Delete a list of global config channels. Caller must be a config admin.

Parameters

- string sessionKey
- array:

    - string - configuration channel labels to delete.

Return Value

- int - 1 on success, exception thrown otherwise.

10.6 deleteFileRevisions

Description

Delete specified revisions of a given configuration file

Parameters

- string sessionKey
- string channelLabel - Label of config channel to lookup on.
- string filePath - Configuration file path.
- array:

    - int - List of revisions to delete

Return Value

- int - 1 on success, exception thrown otherwise.

10.7 deleteFiles

Description

Remove file paths from a global channel.

Parameters

- string sessionKey
- string channelLabel - Channel to remove the files from.
- array:

    - string - file paths to remove.

Return Value

- int - 1 on success, exception thrown otherwise.

10.8 deployAllSystems

Description

Schedule an immediate configuration deployment for all systems subscribed to a particular configuration channel.

Parameters

- string sessionKey
- string channelLabel - The configuration channel's label.

- int - 1 on success, exception thrown otherwise.

10.9 deployAllSystems

Description

Schedule a configuration deployment for all systems subscribed to a particular configuration channel.

Parameters

- string sessionKey
- string channelLabel - The configuration channel's label.
- dateTime.iso8601 date - The date to schedule the action

Return Value

- int - 1 on success, exception thrown otherwise.

10.10 deployAllSystems

Description

Schedule a configuration deployment of a certain file for all systems subscribed to a particular configuration channel.

Parameters

- string sessionKey
- string channelLabel - The configuration channel's label.
- string filePath - The configuration file path.

Return Value

- int - 1 on success, exception thrown otherwise.

10.11 deployAllSystems

Description

Schedule a configuration deployment of a certain file for all systems subscribed to a particular configuration channel.

Parameters

- string sessionKey
- string channelLabel - The configuration channel's label.
- string filePath - The configuration file path.
- dateTime.iso8601 date - The date to schedule the action

Return Value

- int - 1 on success, exception thrown otherwise.

10.12 getDetails

Description

Lookup config channel details.

Parameters

- string sessionKey
- string channelLabel

Return Value

- struct - Configuration Channel information

    - int "id"
    - int "orgId"

- string "label"
- string "name"
- string "description"
- struct "configChannelType"
- struct - Configuration Channel Type information

    - int "id"
    - string "label"
    - string "name"
    - int "priority"

10.13 getDetails

Description

Lookup config channel details.

Parameters

- string sessionKey
- int channelId

Return Value

- struct - Configuration Channel information

    - int "id"
    - int "orgId"
    - string "label"
    - string "name"
    - string "description"
    - struct "configChannelType"
    - struct - Configuration Channel Type information

        - int "id"
        - string "label"

- string "name"
- int "priority"

10.14 getEncodedFileRevision

Description

Get revision of the specified configuration file and transmit the contents as base64 encoded.

Parameters

- string sessionKey
- string configChannelLabel - label of config channel to lookup on
- string filePath - config file path to examine
- int revision - config file revision to examine

Return Value

- struct - Configuration Revision information

  - string "type"
    - file
    - directory
    - symlink
  - string "path" - File Path
  - string "target_path" - Symbolic link Target File Path. Present for Symbolic links only.
  - string "channel" - Channel Name
  - string "contents" - File contents (base64 encoded according to the contents_enc64 attribute)
  - boolean "contents_enc64" - Identifies base64 encoded content
  - int "revision" - File Revision
  - dateTime.iso8601 "creation" - Creation Date
  - dateTime.iso8601 "modified" - Last Modified Date
  - string "owner" - File Owner. Present for files or directories only.
  - string "group" - File Group. Present for files or directories only.
  - int "permissions" - File Permissions (Deprecated). Present for files or directories only.

- string "permissions_mode" - File Permissions. Present for files or directories only.
- string "selinux_ctx" - SELinux Context (optional).
- boolean "binary" - true/false , Present for files only.
- string "sha256" - File's sha256 signature. Present for files only.
- string "macro-start-delimiter" - Macro start delimiter for a config file. Present for text files only.
- string "macro-end-delimiter" - Macro end delimiter for a config file. Present for text files only.

10.15 getFileRevision

Description

Get revision of the specified config file

Parameters

- string sessionKey
- string configChannelLabel - label of config channel to lookup on
- string filePath - config file path to examine
- int revision - config file revision to examine

Return Value

- struct - Configuration Revision information

    - string "type"
        - file
        - directory
        - symlink
    - string "path" - File Path
    - string "target_path" - Symbolic link Target File Path. Present for Symbolic links only.
    - string "channel" - Channel Name
    - string "contents" - File contents (base64 encoded according to the contents_enc64 attribute)
    - boolean "contents_enc64" - Identifies base64 encoded content
    - int "revision" - File Revision
    - dateTime.iso8601 "creation" - Creation Date

- dateTime.iso8601 "modified" - Last Modified Date
- string "owner" - File Owner. Present for files or directories only.
- string "group" - File Group. Present for files or directories only.
- int "permissions" - File Permissions (Deprecated). Present for files or directories only.
- string "permissions_mode" - File Permissions. Present for files or directories only.
- string "selinux_ctx" - SELinux Context (optional).
- boolean "binary" - true/false , Present for files only.
- string "sha256" - File's sha256 signature. Present for files only.
- string "macro-start-delimiter" - Macro start delimiter for a config file. Present for text files only.
- string "macro-end-delimiter" - Macro end delimiter for a config file. Present for text files only.

10.16 getFileRevisions

Description

Get list of revisions for specified config file

Parameters

- string sessionKey
- string channelLabel - label of config channel to lookup on
- string filePath - config file path to examine

Return Value

- array:

    - struct - Configuration Revision information

        - string "type"
            - file
            - directory
            - symlink
        - string "path" - File Path
        - string "target_path" - Symbolic link Target File Path. Present for Symbolic links only.

- string "channel" - Channel Name
- string "contents" - File contents (base64 encoded according to the contents_enc64 attribute)
- boolean "contents_enc64" - Identifies base64 encoded content
- int "revision" - File Revision
- dateTime.iso8601 "creation" - Creation Date
- dateTime.iso8601 "modified" - Last Modified Date
- string "owner" - File Owner. Present for files or directories only.
- string "group" - File Group. Present for files or directories only.
- int "permissions" - File Permissions (Deprecated). Present for files or directories only.
- string "permissions_mode" - File Permissions. Present for files or directories only.
- string "selinux_ctx" - SELinux Context (optional).
- boolean "binary" - true/false , Present for files only.
- string "sha256" - File's sha256 signature. Present for files only.
- string "macro-start-delimiter" - Macro start delimiter for a config file. Present for text files only.
- string "macro-end-delimiter" - Macro end delimiter for a config file. Present for text files only.

10.17 listFiles

Description

Return a list of files in a channel.

Parameters

- string sessionKey
- string channelLabel - label of config channel to list files on.

Return Value

- array:

  - struct - Configuration File information

- string "type"
  - file
    - directory
    - symlink
- string "path" - File Path
- dateTime.iso8601 "last_modified" - Last Modified Date

10.18 listGlobals

Description

List all the global config channels accessible to the logged-in user.

Parameters

- string sessionKey

Return Value

- array:

  - struct - Configuration Channel information

    - int "id"
    - int "orgId"
    - string "label"
    - string "name"
    - string "description"
    - string "type"
    - struct "configChannelType"
    - struct - Configuration Channel Type information

      - int "id"
      - string "label"

- string "name"
- int "priority"

10.19 listSubscribedSystems

Description

Return a list of systems subscribed to a configuration channel

Parameters

- string sessionKey
- string channelLabel - label of config channel to list subscribed systems.

Return Value

- array:

    - struct - system

        - int "id"
        - string "name"

10.20 lookupChannelInfo

Description

Lists details on a list channels given their channel labels.

Parameters

- string sessionKey
- array:

    - string - configuration channel label

Return Value

- array:

    - struct - Configuration Channel information

- int "id"
- int "orgId"
- string "label"
- string "name"
- string "description"
- struct "configChannelType"
- struct - Configuration Channel Type information

  - int "id"
  - string "label"
  - string "name"
  - int "priority"

10.21 lookupFileInfo

Description

Given a list of paths and a channel, returns details about the latest revisions of the paths.
Available since: 10.2

Parameters

- string sessionKey
- string channelLabel - label of config channel to lookup on
- array:

  - string - List of paths to examine.

Return Value

- array:

  - struct - Configuration Revision information

    - string "type"
      - file
      - directory
      - symlink
    - string "path" - File Path

- string "target_path" - Symbolic link Target File Path. Present for Symbolic links only.
- string "channel" - Channel Name
- string "contents" - File contents (base64 encoded according to the contents_enc64 attribute)
- boolean "contents_enc64" - Identifies base64 encoded content
- int "revision" - File Revision
- dateTime.iso8601 "creation" - Creation Date
- dateTime.iso8601 "modified" - Last Modified Date
- string "owner" - File Owner. Present for files or directories only.
- string "group" - File Group. Present for files or directories only.
- int "permissions" - File Permissions (Deprecated). Present for files or directories only.
- string "permissions_mode" - File Permissions. Present for files or directories only.
- string "selinux_ctx" - SELinux Context (optional).
- boolean "binary" - true/false , Present for files only.
- string "sha256" - File's sha256 signature. Present for files only.
- string "macro-start-delimiter" - Macro start delimiter for a config file. Present for text files only.
- string "macro-end-delimiter" - Macro end delimiter for a config file. Present for text files only.

10.22 lookupFileInfo

Description

Given a path, revision number, and a channel, returns details about the latest revisions of the paths.

Available since: 10.12

Parameters

- string sessionKey
- string channelLabel - label of config channel to lookup on
- string path - path of file/directory
- int revsion - The revision number.

Return Value

- struct - Configuration Revision information

  - string "type"
    - file
      - directory
      - symlink
  - string "path" - File Path
  - string "target_path" - Symbolic link Target File Path. Present for Symbolic links only.
  - string "channel" - Channel Name
  - string "contents" - File contents (base64 encoded according to the contents_enc64 attribute)
  - boolean "contents_enc64" - Identifies base64 encoded content
  - int "revision" - File Revision
  - dateTime.iso8601 "creation" - Creation Date
  - dateTime.iso8601 "modified" - Last Modified Date
  - string "owner" - File Owner. Present for files or directories only.
  - string "group" - File Group. Present for files or directories only.
  - int "permissions" - File Permissions (Deprecated). Present for files or directories only.
  - string "permissions_mode" - File Permissions. Present for files or directories only.
  - string "selinux_ctx" - SELinux Context (optional).
  - boolean "binary" - true/false , Present for files only.
  - string "sha256" - File's sha256 signature. Present for files only.
  - string "macro-start-delimiter" - Macro start delimiter for a config file. Present for text files only.
  - string "macro-end-delimiter" - Macro end delimiter for a config file. Present for text files only.

10.23 scheduleFileComparisons

Description

Schedule a comparison of the latest revision of a file against the version deployed on a list of systems.

Parameters

- string sessionKey
- string channelLabel - Label of config channel
- string path - File path
- array:

    - long - The list of server id that the comparison will be performed on

Return Value

- int actionId - The action id of the scheduled action

10.24 update

Description

Update a global config channel. Caller must be at least a config admin or an organization admin, or have access to a system containing this config channel.

Parameters

- string sessionKey
- string channelLabel
- string channelName
- string description

Return Value

- struct - Configuration Channel information

    - int "id"
    - int "orgId"
    - string "label"
    - string "name"
    - string "description"
    - struct "configChannelType"
    - struct - Configuration Channel Type information

        - int "id"
        - string "label"

- string "name"
- int "priority"

11 distchannel

Provides methods to access and modify distribution channel information

11.1 listDefaultMaps

Description

> Lists the default distribution channel maps

Parameters

> - string sessionKey

Return Value

> - array:
>
>   - struct - distChannelMap
>
>   - string "os" - Operationg System
>   - string "release" - OS Relase
>   - string "arch_name" - Channel architecture
>   - string "channel_label" - Channel label
>   - string "org_specific" - 'Y' organization specific, 'N' default

11.2 listMapsForOrg

Description

> Lists distribution channel maps valid for the user's organization

Parameters

> - string sessionKey

Return Value

> - array:
>
>   - struct - distChannelMap

- string "os" - Operationg System
- string "release" - OS Relase
- string "arch_name" - Channel architecture
- string "channel_label" - Channel label
- string "org_specific" - 'Y' organization specific, 'N' default

11.3 listMapsForOrg

Description

Lists distribution channel maps valid for an organization, satellite admin right needed

Parameters

- string sessionKey
- int orgId

Return Value

- array:

    - struct - distChannelMap

        - string "os" - Operationg System
        - string "release" - OS Relase
        - string "arch_name" - Channel architecture
        - string "channel_label" - Channel label
        - string "org_specific" - 'Y' organization specific, 'N' default

11.4 setMapForOrg

Description

Sets, overrides (/removes if channelLabel empty) a distribution channel map within an organization

Parameters

- string sessionKey
- string os

- string release
- string archName
- string channelLabel

Return Value

- int - 1 on success, exception thrown otherwise.

12 errata

Provides methods to access and modify errata.

12.1 addPackages

Description

Add a set of packages to an erratum with the given advisory name. This method will only allow for modification of custom errata created either through the UI or API.

Parameters

- string sessionKey
- string advisoryName
- array:

    - int - packageId

Return Value

- int - representing the number of packages added, exception otherwise

12.2 applicableToChannels

Description

Returns a list of channels applicable to the erratum with the given advisory name.

Parameters

- string sessionKey
- string advisoryName

Return Value

- array:

    - struct - channel

- int "channel_id"
- string "label"
- string "name"
- string "parent_channel_label"

12.3 bugzillaFixes

Description

Get the Bugzilla fixes for an erratum matching the given advisoryName. The bugs will be returned in a struct where the bug id is the key. i.e. 208144 = "errata.bugzillaFixes Method Returns different results than docs say"

Parameters

- string sessionKey
- string advisoryName

Return Value

- struct - Bugzilla info

  - string "bugzilla_id" - actual bug number is the key into the struct
  - string "bug_summary" - summary who's key is the bug id

12.4 clone

Description

Clone a list of errata into the specified channel.

Parameters

- string sessionKey
- string channel_label
- array:

  - string - advisory - The advisory name of the errata to clone.

Return Value

- array:

  - struct - errata

    - int "id" - Errata Id
    - string "date" - Date erratum was created.
    - string "advisory_type" - Type of the advisory.
    - string "advisory_name" - Name of the advisory.
    - string "advisory_synopsis" - Summary of the erratum.

12.5 cloneAsOriginal

Description

Clones a list of errata into a specified cloned channel according the original erratas.

Parameters

- string sessionKey
- string channel_label
- array:

  - string - advisory - The advisory name of the errata to clone.

Return Value

- array:

  - struct - errata

    - int "id" - Errata Id
    - string "date" - Date erratum was created.

- string "advisory_type" - Type of the advisory.
- string "advisory_name" - Name of the advisory.
- string "advisory_synopsis" - Summary of the erratum.

12.6 cloneAsOriginalAsync

Description

Asynchronously clones a list of errata into a specified cloned channel according the original erratas

Parameters

- string sessionKey
- string channel_label
- array:

  - string - advisory - The advisory name of the errata to clone.

Return Value

- int - 1 on success, exception thrown otherwise.

12.7 cloneAsync

Description

Asynchronously clone a list of errata into the specified channel.

Parameters

- string sessionKey
- string channel_label
- array:

    - string - advisory - The advisory name of the errata to clone.

Return Value

- int - 1 on success, exception thrown otherwise.

12.8   create

Description

Create a custom errata. If "publish" is set to true, the errata will be published as well

Parameters

- string sessionKey
- struct - errata info

    - string "synopsis"
    - string "advisory_name"
    - int "advisory_release"
    - string "advisory_type" - Type of advisory (one of the following: 'Security Advisory', 'Product Enhancement Advisory', or 'Bug Fix Advisory'
    - string "product"
    - string "errataFrom"
    - string "topic"
    - string "description"
    - string "references"
    - string "notes"
    - string "solution"
- array:

    - struct - bug

- int "id" - Bug Id
- string "summary"
- string "url"

- array:

    - string - keyword - List of keywords to associate with the errata.
- array:

    - int - packageId
- boolean publish - Should the errata be published.
- array:

    - string - channelLabel - list of channels the errata should be published too, ignored if publish is set to false

Return Value

- struct - errata

    - int "id" - Errata Id
    - string "date" - Date erratum was created.
    - string "advisory_type" - Type of the advisory.
    - string "advisory_name" - Name of the advisory.
    - string "advisory_synopsis" - Summary of the erratum.

12.9 delete

Description

Delete an erratum. This method will only allow for deletion of custom errata created either through the UI or API.

Parameters

- string sessionKey
- string advisoryName

Return Value

- int - 1 on success, exception thrown otherwise.

12.10 findByCve

Description

Lookup the details for errata associated with the given CVE (e.g. CVE-2008-3270)

Parameters

- string sessionKey
- string cveName

Return Value

- array:

    - struct - errata

        - int "id" - Errata Id
        - string "date" - Date erratum was created.
        - string "advisory_type" - Type of the advisory.
        - string "advisory_name" - Name of the advisory.
        - string "advisory_synopsis" - Summary of the erratum.

12.11 getDetails

Description

Retrieves the details for the erratum matching the given advisory name.

Parameters

- string sessionKey
- string advisoryName

Return Value

- struct - erratum

- int "id"
- string "issue_date"
- string "update_date"
- string "last_modified_date" - This date is only included for published erratum and it represents the last time the erratum was modified.
- string "synopsis"
- int "release"
- string "type"
- string "product"
- string "errataFrom"
- string "topic"
- string "description"
- string "references"
- string "notes"
- string "solution"

12.12 listAffectedSystems

Description

Return the list of systems affected by the erratum with advisory name.

Parameters

- string sessionKey
- string advisoryName

Return Value

- array:

    - struct - system

        - int "id"
        - string "name"
        - dateTime.iso8601 "last_checkin" - Last time server successfully checked in
        - dateTime.iso8601 "created" - Server registration time
        - dateTime.iso8601 "last_boot" - Last server boot time

- int "extra_pkg_count" - Number of packages not belonging to any assigned channel
- int "outdated_pkg_count" - Number of out-of-date packages

12.13 listByDate

Description

List errata that have been applied to a particular channel by date.

Deprecated - being replaced by channel.software.listErrata(User LoggedInUser, string channelLabel)

Parameters

- string sessionKey
- string channelLabel

Return Value

- array:

    - struct - errata

        - int "id" - Errata Id
        - string "date" - Date erratum was created.
        - string "advisory_type" - Type of the advisory.
        - string "advisory_name" - Name of the advisory.
        - string "advisory_synopsis" - Summary of the erratum.

12.14 listCves

Description

Returns a list of CVEs applicable to the erratum with the given advisory name. CVEs may be associated only with published errata.

Parameters

- string sessionKey
- string advisoryName

Return Value

- array:

  - string - cveName

12.15 listKeywords

Description

Get the keywords associated with an erratum matching the given advisory name.

Parameters

- string sessionKey
- string advisoryName

Return Value

- array:

  - string - Keyword associated with erratum.

12.16 listPackages

Description

Returns a list of the packages affected by the erratum with the given advisory name.

Parameters

- string sessionKey
- string advisoryName

Return Value

- array:

  - struct - package

    - int "id"
    - string "name"

- string "epoch"
- string "version"
- string "release"
- string "arch_label"
- array "providing_channels"

  - string - - Channel label providing this package.
- string "build_host"
- string "description"
- string "checksum"
- string "checksum_type"
- string "vendor"
- string "summary"
- string "cookie"
- string "license"
- string "path"
- string "file"
- string "build_date"
- string "last_modified_date"
- string "size"
- string "payload_size"

12.17 listUnpublishedErrata

Description

Returns a list of unpublished errata

Parameters

- string sessionKey

Return Value

- array:

  - struct - erratum

- int "id"
- int "published"
- string "advisory"
- string "advisory_name"
- string "advisory_type"
- string "synopsis"
- dateTime.iso8601 "created"
- dateTime.iso8601 "update_date"

12.18 publish

Description

> Publish an existing (unpublished) errata to a set of channels.

Parameters

- string sessionKey
- string advisoryName
- array:

    - string - channelLabel - list of channel labels to publish to

Return Value

- struct - errata

    - int "id" - Errata Id
    - string "date" - Date erratum was created.
    - string "advisory_type" - Type of the advisory.
    - string "advisory_name" - Name of the advisory.
    - string "advisory_synopsis" - Summary of the erratum.

12.19 publishAsOriginal

Description

> Publishes an existing (unpublished) cloned errata to a set of cloned channels according to its original erratum

Parameters

- string sessionKey
- string advisoryName
- array:

    - string - channelLabel - list of channel labels to publish to

Return Value

- struct - errata

    - int "id" - Errata Id
    - string "date" - Date erratum was created.
    - string "advisory_type" - Type of the advisory.
    - string "advisory_name" - Name of the advisory.
    - string "advisory_synopsis" - Summary of the erratum.

12.20 removePackages

Description

Remove a set of packages from an erratum with the given advisory name. This method will only allow for modification of custom errata created either through the UI or API.

Parameters

- string sessionKey
- string advisoryName
- array:

    - int - packageId

Return Value

- int - representing the number of packages removed, exception otherwise

12.21 setDetails

Description

Set erratum details. All arguments are optional and will only be modified if included in the struct. This method will only allow for modification of custom errata created either through the UI or API.

Parameters

- string sessionKey
- string advisoryName
- struct - errata details

    - string "synopsis"
    - string "advisory_name"
    - int "advisory_release"
    - string "advisory_type" - Type of advisory (one of the following: 'Security Advisory', 'Product Enhancement Advisory', or 'Bug Fix Advisory'
    - string "product"
    - dateTime.iso8601 "issue_date"
    - dateTime.iso8601 "update_date"
    - string "errataFrom"
    - string "topic"
    - string "description"
    - string "references"
    - string "notes"

- string "solution"
- array "bugs" - 'bugs' is the key into the struct
- array:

    - struct - bug

        - int "id" - Bug Id
        - string "summary"
        - string "url"
- array "keywords" - 'keywords' is the key into the struct
- array:

    - string - keyword - List of keywords to associate with the errata.
- array "CVEs" - 'cves' is the key into the struct
- array:

    - string - cves - List of CVEs to associate with the errata. (valid only for published errata)

Return Value

- int - 1 on success, exception thrown otherwise.

13 formula

Provides methods to access and modify formulas.

13.1 getCombinedFormulasByServerId

Description

> Return the list of formulas a server and all his groups have.

Parameters

- string sessionKey
- int systemId

Return Value

- array:

  - string - (formulas)

13.2 getFormulasByGroupId

Description

> Return the list of formulas a server group has.

Parameters

- string sessionKey
- int systemGroupId

Return Value

- array:

    - string - (formulas)

13.3 getFormulasByServerId

Description

Return the list of formulas directly applied to a server.

Parameters

- string sessionKey
- int systemId

Return Value

- array:

    - string - (formulas)

13.4 listFormulas

Description

Return the list of formulas currently installed.

Parameters

- string sessionKey

Return Value

- array:

    - string - (formulas)

13.5 setFormulasOfGroup

Description

Set the formulas of a server group.

Parameters

- string sessionKey
- int systemGroupId
- array:

    - string - formulaName

Return Value

- int - 1 on success, exception thrown otherwise.

13.6 setFormulasOfServer

Description

Set the formulas of a server.

Parameters

- string sessionKey
- int systemId
- array:
    - string - formulaName

Return Value

- int - 1 on success, exception thrown otherwise.

14 image

Provides methods to access and modify images.

14.1 delete

Description

Delete an Image

Parameters

- string sessionKey
- int imageId

Return Value

- int - 1 on success, exception thrown otherwise.

14.2 getCustomValues

Description

Get the custom data values defined for the Image.

Parameters

- string sessionKey
- int imageId

Return Value

- struct - Map of custom labels to custom values

- string "custom info label"
- string "value"

14.3 getDetails

Description

Get details of an Image

Parameters

- string sessionKey
- int imageId

Return Value

- struct - Image Overview information
  - int "id"
  - string "name" - image name
  - string "version" - image tag/version
  - int "revision" - image build revision number
  - string "arch" - image architecture
  - boolean "external" - true if the image is built externally, false otherwise
  - string "checksum"
  - string "profileLabel"
  - string "buildStatus" - One of:
    - queued
    - picked up
    - completed
    - failed
  - string "inspectStatus" - Available if the build is successful. One of:
    - queued
    - picked up
    - completed
    - failed
  - int "buildServerId"
  - int "securityErrata"

- int "bugErrata"
- int "enhancementErrata"
- int "outdatedPackages"
- int "installedPackages"

14.4 getRelevantErrata

Description

Returns a list of all errata that are relevant for the image

Parameters

- string sessionKey
- int imageId

Return Value

- array:

  - struct - errata

    - int "id" - Errata ID.
    - string "date" - Date erratum was created.
    - string "update_date" - Date erratum was updated.
    - string "advisory_synopsis" - Summary of the erratum.
    - string "advisory_type" - Type label such as Security, Bug Fix
    - string "advisory_name" - Name such as RHSA, etc

14.5 importImage

Description

Import an image and schedule an inspect afterwards

Parameters

- string sessionKey
- string name - image name as specified in the store
- string version - version to import or empty

- int buildHostId - system ID of the build host
- string storeLabel
- string activationKey - activation key to get the channel data from
- dateTime.iso8601 earliestOccurrence - earliest the following inspect can run

Return Value

- int - ID of the inspect action created

14.6 listImages

Description

List available Images

Parameters

- string sessionKey

Return Value

- array:

    - struct - Image information

        - int "id"
        - string "name" - image name
        - string "version" - image tag/version
        - int "revision" - image build revision number
        - string "arch" - image architecture
        - boolean "external" - true if the image is built externally, false otherwise
        - string "storeLabel"
        - string "checksum"

14.7 listPackages

Description

List the installed packages on the given image.

Parameters

- string sessionKey
- int imageId

Return Value

- array:

    - struct - package

        - string "name"
        - string "version"
        - string "release"
        - string "epoch"
        - string "arch"

14.8 scheduleImageBuild

Description

Schedule an image build

Parameters

- string sessionKey
- string profileLabel
- string version - version to build or empty
- int buildHostId - system id of the build host
- dateTime.iso8601 earliestOccurrence - earliest the build can run.

Return Value

- int - ID of the build action created.

15 image.profile

Provides methods to access and modify image profiles.

15.1 create

Description

Create a new Image Profile

Parameters

- string sessionKey
- string label
- string type
- string storeLabel
- string path
- string activationKey - Optional

Return Value

- int - 1 on success, exception thrown otherwise.

15.2 delete

Description

Delete an Image Profile

Parameters

- string sessionKey
- string label

Return Value

- int - 1 on success, exception thrown otherwise.

15.3 deleteCustomValues

Description

Delete the custom values defined for the specified Image Profile.
(Note: Attempt to delete values of non-existing keys throws exception. Attempt to delete value of existing key which has assigned no values doesn't throw exception.)

Parameters

- string sessionKey
- string label
- array:

  - string - customDataKeys

Return Value

- int - 1 on success, exception thrown otherwise.

15.4 getCustomValues

Description

Get the custom data values defined for the Image Profile.

Parameters

- string sessionKey
- string label

Return Value

- struct - Map of custom labels to custom values

- string "custom info label"
- string "value"

15.5 getDetails

Description

Get details of an Image Profile

Parameters

- string sessionKey
- string label

Return Value

- struct - Image Profile information

  - string "label"
  - string "imageType"
  - string "imageStore"
  - string "activationKey"
  - string "path" - in case type support path

15.6 listImageProfileTypes

Description

List available Image Store Types

Parameters

- string sessionKey

Return Value

- array:

  - string - imageProfileTypes

15.7 listImageProfiles

Description

List available Image Profiles

Parameters

- string sessionKey

Return Value

- array:

  - struct - Image Profile information

    - string "label"
    - string "imageType"
    - string "imageStore"
    - string "activationKey"
    - string "path" - in case type support path

15.8 setCustomValues

Description

Set custom values for the specified Image Profile.

Parameters

- string sessionKey
- string label
- struct - Map of custom labels to custom values

    - string "custom info label"
    - string "value"

Return Value

- int - 1 on success, exception thrown otherwise.

15.9 setDetails

Description

Set details of an Image Profile

Parameters

- string sessionKey
- string label
- struct - image profile details

    - string "storeLabel"
    - string "path"
    - string "activationKey" - set empty string to unset

Return Value

- int - 1 on success, exception thrown otherwise.

16 image.store

Provides methods to access and modify image stores.

16.1 create

Description

> Create a new Image Store

Parameters

- string sessionKey
- string label
- string uri
- string storeType
- struct - credentials optional

  - string "username"
  - string "password"

Return Value

- int - 1 on success, exception thrown otherwise.

16.2 delete

Description

> Delete an Image Store

Parameters

- string sessionKey
- string label

Return Value

- int - 1 on success, exception thrown otherwise.

16.3   getDetails

Description

Get details of an Image Store

Parameters

- string sessionKey
- string label

Return Value

- struct - Image Store information

    - string "label"
    - string "uri"
    - string "storetype"
    - boolean "hasCredentials"
    - string "username"

16.4   listImageStoreTypes

Description

List available Image Store Types

Parameters

- string sessionKey

Return Value

- array:

    - struct - Image Store Type information

- int "id"
- string "label"
- string "name"

16.5 listImageStores

Description

List available Image Stores

Parameters

- string sessionKey

Return Value

- array:

  - struct - Image Store information

    - string "label"
    - string "uri"
    - string "storetype"
    - boolean "hasCredentials"
    - string "username"

16.6 setDetails

Description

Set details of an Image Store

Parameters

- string sessionKey
- string label
- struct - image store details

- string "uri"
- string "username" - pass empty string to unset credentials
- string "password"

Return Value

- int - 1 on success, exception thrown otherwise.

17 kickstart

Provides methods to create kickstart files

17.1 cloneProfile

Description

Clone a Kickstart Profile

Parameters

- string sessionKey
- string ksLabelToClone - Label of the kickstart profile to clone
- string newKsLabel - label of the cloned profile

Return Value

- int - 1 on success, exception thrown otherwise.

17.2 createProfile

Description

Import a kickstart profile.

Parameters

- string sessionKey
- string profileLabel - Label for the new kickstart profile.
- string virtualizationType - none, para_host, qemu, xenfv or xenpv.
- string kickstartableTreeLabel - Label of a kickstartable tree to associate the new profile with.
- string kickstartHost - Kickstart hostname (of a satellite or proxy) used to construct the default download URL for the new kickstart profile.
- string rootPassword - Root password.
- string updateType - Should the profile update itself to use the newest tree available? Possible values are: none (default) or all (includes custom Kickstart Trees).

Return Value

- int - 1 on success, exception thrown otherwise.

17.3 createProfile

Description

Import a kickstart profile.

Parameters

- string sessionKey
- string profileLabel - Label for the new kickstart profile.
- string virtualizationType - none, para_host, qemu, xenfv or xenpv.
- string kickstartableTreeLabel - Label of a kickstartable tree to associate the new profile with.
- string kickstartHost - Kickstart hostname (of a satellite or proxy) used to construct the default download URL for the new kickstart profile.
- string rootPassword - Root password.

Return Value

- int - 1 on success, exception thrown otherwise.

17.4 createProfileWithCustomUrl

Description

Import a kickstart profile.

Parameters

- string sessionKey
- string profileLabel - Label for the new kickstart profile.
- string virtualizationType - none, para_host, qemu, xenfv or xenpv.
- string kickstartableTreeLabel - Label of a kickstartable tree to associate the new profile with.

- boolean downloadUrl - Download URL, or 'default' to use the kickstart tree's default URL.
- string rootPassword - Root password.

Return Value

- int - 1 on success, exception thrown otherwise.

17.5 createProfileWithCustomUrl

Description

Import a kickstart profile.

Parameters

- string sessionKey
- string profileLabel - Label for the new kickstart profile.
- string virtualizationType - none, para_host, qemu, xenfv or xenpv.
- string kickstartableTreeLabel - Label of a kickstartable tree to associate the new profile with.
- boolean downloadUrl - Download URL, or 'default' to use the kickstart tree's default URL.
- string rootPassword - Root password.
- string updateType - Should the profile update itself to use the newest tree available? Possible values are: none (default) or all (includes custom Kickstart Trees).

Return Value

- int - 1 on success, exception thrown otherwise.

17.6 deleteProfile

Description

Delete a kickstart profile

Parameters

- string sessionKey
- string ksLabel - The label of the kickstart profile you want to remove

Return Value

- int - 1 on success, exception thrown otherwise.

17.7 disableProfile

Description

Enable/Disable a Kickstart Profile

Parameters

- string sessionKey
- string profileLabel - Label for the kickstart tree you want to en/disable
- string disabled - true to disable the profile

Return Value

- int - 1 on success, exception thrown otherwise.

17.8 findKickstartForIp

Description

Find an associated kickstart for a given ip address.

Parameters

- string sessionKey
- string ipAddress - The ip address to search for (i.e. 192.168.0.1)

Return Value

- string - label of the kickstart. Empty string ("") if not found.

17.9 importFile

Description

Import a kickstart profile.

Parameters

- string sessionKey
- string profileLabel - Label for the new kickstart profile.
- string virtualizationType - none, para_host, qemu, xenfv or xenpv.
- string kickstartableTreeLabel - Label of a kickstartable tree to associate the new profile with.
- string kickstartFileContents - Contents of the kickstart file to import.

Return Value

- int - 1 on success, exception thrown otherwise.

17.10 importFile

Description

Import a kickstart profile.

Parameters

- string sessionKey
- string profileLabel - Label for the new kickstart profile.
- string virtualizationType - none, para_host, qemu, xenfv or xenpv.
- string kickstartableTreeLabel - Label of a kickstartable tree to associate the new profile with.

- string kickstartHost - Kickstart hostname (of a satellite or proxy) used to construct the default download URL for the new kickstart profile. Using this option signifies that this default URL will be used instead of any url/nfs/cdrom/harddrive commands in the kickstart file itself.
- string kickstartFileContents - Contents of the kickstart file to import.

Return Value

- int - 1 on success, exception thrown otherwise.

17.11 importFile

Description

Import a kickstart profile.

Parameters

- string sessionKey
- string profileLabel - Label for the new kickstart profile.
- string virtualizationType - none, para_host, qemu, xenfv or xenpv.
- string kickstartableTreeLabel - Label of a kickstartable tree to associate the new profile with.
- string kickstartHost - Kickstart hostname (of a satellite or proxy) used to construct the default download URL for the new kickstart profile. Using this option signifies that this default URL will be used instead of any url/nfs/cdrom/harddrive commands in the kickstart file itself.
- string kickstartFileContents - Contents of the kickstart file to import.
- string updateType - Should the profile update itself to use the newest tree available? Possible values are: none (default) or all (includes custom Kickstart Trees).

Return Value

- int - 1 on success, exception thrown otherwise.

17.12 importRawFile

Description

Import a raw kickstart file into satellite.

Parameters

- string sessionKey
- string profileLabel - Label for the new kickstart profile.
- string virtualizationType - none, para_host, qemu, xenfv or xenpv.
- string kickstartableTreeLabel - Label of a kickstartable tree to associate the new profile with.
- string kickstartFileContents - Contents of the kickstart file to import.

Return Value

- int - 1 on success, exception thrown otherwise.

17.13 importRawFile

Description

Import a raw kickstart file into satellite.

Parameters

- string sessionKey
- string profileLabel - Label for the new kickstart profile.
- string virtualizationType - none, para_host, qemu, xenfv or xenpv.
- string kickstartableTreeLabel - Label of a kickstartable tree to associate the new profile with.
- string kickstartFileContents - Contents of the kickstart file to import.
- string updateType - Should the profile update itself to use the newest tree available? Possible values are: none (default) or all (includes custom Kickstart Trees).

Return Value

- int - 1 on success, exception thrown otherwise.

17.14 isProfileDisabled

Description

Returns whether a kickstart profile is disabled

Parameters

- string sessionKey
- string profileLabel - kickstart profile label

Return Value

- true if profile is disabled

17.15 listAllIpRanges

Description

List all Ip Ranges and their associated kickstarts available in the user's org.

Parameters

- string sessionKey

Return Value

- array:
    - struct - Kickstart Ip Range

- string "ksLabel" - The kickstart label associated with the ip range
- string "max" - The max ip of the range
- string "min" - The min ip of the range

17.16 listAutoinstallableChannels

Description

List autoinstallable channels for the logged in user.

Parameters

- string sessionKey

Return Value

- array:

  - struct - channel

    - int "id"
    - string "name"
    - string "label"
    - string "arch_name"
    - string "arch_label"
    - string "summary"
    - string "description"
    - string "checksum_label"
    - dateTime.iso8601 "last_modified"
    - string "maintainer_name"
    - string "maintainer_email"
    - string "maintainer_phone"
    - string "support_policy"
    - string "gpg_key_url"
    - string "gpg_key_id"
    - string "gpg_key_fp"
    - dateTime.iso8601 "yumrepo_last_sync" - (optional)
    - string "end_of_life"

- string "parent_channel_label"
- string "clone_original"
- array:

    - struct - contentSources

        - int "id"
        - string "label"
        - string "sourceUrl"
        - string "type"

17.17 listKickstartableChannels

Description

List kickstartable channels for the logged in user.

Parameters

- string sessionKey

Return Value

- array:

    - struct - channel

        - int "id"
        - string "name"
        - string "label"
        - string "arch_name"
        - string "arch_label"
        - string "summary"
        - string "description"
        - string "checksum_label"
        - dateTime.iso8601 "last_modified"
        - string "maintainer_name"
        - string "maintainer_email"
        - string "maintainer_phone"

- string "support_policy"
- string "gpg_key_url"
- string "gpg_key_id"
- string "gpg_key_fp"
- dateTime.iso8601 "yumrepo_last_sync" - (optional)
- string "end_of_life"
- string "parent_channel_label"
- string "clone_original"
- array:

    - struct - contentSources

        - int "id"
        - string "label"
        - string "sourceUrl"
        - string "type"

17.18 listKickstartableTrees

Description

List the available kickstartable trees for the given channel.

Deprecated - being replaced by kickstart.tree.list(string sessionKey, string channelLabel)

Parameters

- string sessionKey
- string channelLabel - Label of channel to search.

Return Value

- array:

    - struct - kickstartable tree

        - int "id"
        - string "label"

- string "base_path"
- int "channel_id"

17.19 listKickstarts

Description

Provides a list of kickstart profiles visible to the user's org

Parameters

- string sessionKey

Return Value

- array:

  - struct - kickstart

    - string "label"
    - string "tree_label"
    - string "name"
    - boolean "advanced_mode"
    - boolean "org_default"
    - boolean "active"
    - string "update_type"

17.20 renameProfile

Description

Rename a Kickstart Profile in Satellite

Parameters

- string sessionKey
- string originalLabel - Label for the kickstart profile you want to rename
- string newLabel - new label to change to

Return Value

- int - 1 on success, exception thrown otherwise.

renameProfile   SUSE Manager 3.1

18 kickstart.filepreservation

Provides methods to retrieve and manipulate kickstart file preservation lists.

18.1 create

Description

Create a new file preservation list.

Parameters

- string session_key
- string name - name of the file list to create
- array:
    - string - name - file names to include

Return Value

- int - 1 on success, exception thrown otherwise.

18.2 delete

Description

Delete a file preservation list.

Parameters

- string session_key
- string name - name of the file list to delete

Return Value

- int - 1 on success, exception thrown otherwise.

18.3 getDetails

Description

Returns all of the data associated with the given file preservation list.

Parameters

- string session_key
- string name - name of the file list to retrieve details for

Return Value

- struct - file list

    - string "name"
    - array "file_names"

        - string - name

18.4 listAllFilePreservations

Description

List all file preservation lists for the organization associated with the user logged into the given session

Parameters

- string sessionKey

Return Value

- array:

    - struct - file preservation

- int "id"
- string "name"
- dateTime.iso8601 "created"
- dateTime.iso8601 "last_modified"

19 kickstart.keys

Provides methods to manipulate kickstart keys.

19.1 create

Description

creates a new key with the given parameters

Parameters

- string session_key
- string description
- string type - valid values are GPG or SSL
- string content

Return Value

- int - 1 on success, exception thrown otherwise.

19.2 delete

Description

deletes the key identified by the given parameters

Parameters

- string session_key
- string description

Return Value

- int - 1 on success, exception thrown otherwise.

19.3 getDetails

Description

returns all of the data associated with the given key

Parameters

- string session_key
- string description

Return Value

- struct - key

    - string "description"
    - string "type"
    - string "content"

19.4 listAllKeys

Description

list all keys for the org associated with the user logged into the given session

Parameters

- string sessionKey

Return Value

- array:

    - struct - key

        - string "description"
        - string "type"

19.5 update

Description

Updates type and content of the key identified by the description

Parameters

- string session_key
- string description

- string type - valid values are GPG or SSL
- string content

Return Value

- int - 1 on success, exception thrown otherwise.

20   kickstart.profile

Provides methods to access and modify many aspects of a kickstart profile.

20.1   addIpRange

Description

> Add an ip range to a kickstart profile.

Parameters

- string sessionKey
- string label - The label of the kickstart
- string min - The ip address making up the minimum of the range (i.e. 192.168.0.1)
- string max - The ip address making up the maximum of the range (i.e. 192.168.0.254)

Return Value

- int - 1 on success, exception thrown otherwise.

20.2   addScript

Description

> Add a pre/post script to a kickstart profile.

Parameters

- string sessionKey
- string ksLabel - The kickstart label to add the script to.
- string name - The kickstart script name.
- string contents - The full script to add.
- string interpreter - The path to the interpreter to use (i.e. /bin/bash). An empty string will use the kickstart default interpreter.
- string type - The type of script (either 'pre' or 'post').
- boolean chroot - Whether to run the script in the chrooted install location (recommended) or not.

Return Value

- int id - the id of the added script

20.3 addScript

Description

Add a pre/post script to a kickstart profile.

Parameters

- string sessionKey
- string ksLabel - The kickstart label to add the script to.
- string name - The kickstart script name.
- string contents - The full script to add.
- string interpreter - The path to the interpreter to use (i.e. /bin/bash). An empty string will use the kickstart default interpreter.
- string type - The type of script (either 'pre' or 'post').
- boolean chroot - Whether to run the script in the chrooted install location (recommended) or not.
- boolean template - Enable templating using cobbler.

Return Value

- int id - the id of the added script

20.4 addScript

Description

Add a pre/post script to a kickstart profile.

Parameters

- string sessionKey
- string ksLabel - The kickstart label to add the script to.
- string name - The kickstart script name.
- string contents - The full script to add.

- string interpreter - The path to the interpreter to use (i.e. /bin/bash). An empty string will use the kickstart default interpreter.
- string type - The type of script (either 'pre' or 'post').
- boolean chroot - Whether to run the script in the chrooted install location (recommended) or not.
- boolean template - Enable templating using cobbler.
- boolean erroronfail - Whether to throw an error if the script fails or not

Return Value

- int id - the id of the added script

20.5 compareActivationKeys

Description

Returns a list for each kickstart profile; each list will contain activation keys not present on the other profile.

Parameters

- string sessionKey
- string kickstartLabel1
- string kickstartLabel2

Return Value

- struct - Comparison Info

    - array "kickstartLabel1" - Actual label of the first kickstart profile is the key into the struct
    - array:

        - struct - activation key

            - string "key"
            - string "description"
            - int "usage_limit"
            - string "base_channel_label"
            - array "child_channel_labels"

- string - childChannelLabel
- array "entitlements"

  - string - entitlementLabel
- array "server_group_ids"

  - string - serverGroupId
- array "package_names"

  - string - packageName - (deprecated by packages)
- array "packages"

  - struct - package

    - string "name" - packageName
    - string "arch" - archLabel - optional
- boolean "universal_default"
- boolean "disabled"
- string "contact_method" - One of the following:
  - default
  - ssh-push
  - ssh-push-tunnel
- array "kickstartLabel2" - Actual label of the second kickstart profile is the key into the struct
- array:

  - struct - activation key

    - string "key"
    - string "description"
    - int "usage_limit"
    - string "base_channel_label"
    - array "child_channel_labels"

      - string - childChannelLabel
    - array "entitlements"

      - string - entitlementLabel
    - array "server_group_ids"

- string - serverGroupId
- array "package_names"

  - string - packageName - (deprecated by packages)
- array "packages"

  - struct - package

    - string "name" - packageName
    - string "arch" - archLabel - optional
- boolean "universal_default"
- boolean "disabled"
- string "contact_method" - One of the following:
  - default
  - ssh-push
  - ssh-push-tunnel

20.6 compareAdvancedOptions

Description

Returns a list for each kickstart profile; each list will contain the properties that differ between the profiles and their values for that specific profile .

Parameters

- string sessionKey
- string kickstartLabel1
- string kickstartLabel2

Return Value

- struct - Comparison Info

  - array "kickstartLabel1" - Actual label of the first kickstart profile is the key into the struct
  - array:

    - struct - value

- string "name"
- string "value"
- boolean "enabled"
- array "kickstartLabel2" - Actual label of the second kickstart profile is the key into the struct
- array:

  - struct - value

    - string "name"
    - string "value"
    - boolean "enabled"

20.7   comparePackages

Description

Returns a list for each kickstart profile; each list will contain package names not present on the other profile.

Parameters

- string sessionKey
- string kickstartLabel1
- string kickstartLabel2

Return Value

- struct - Comparison Info

- array "kickstartLabel1" - Actual label of the first kickstart profile is the key into the struct
- array:

    - string - package name
- array "kickstartLabel2" - Actual label of the second kickstart profile is the key into the struct
- array:

    - string - package name

20.8 downloadKickstart

Description

Download the full contents of a kickstart file.

Parameters

- string sessionKey
- string ksLabel - The label of the kickstart to download.
- string host - The host to use when referring to the satellite itself (Usually this should be the FQDN of the satellite, but could be the ip address or shortname of it as well.

Return Value

- string - The contents of the kickstart file. Note: if an activation key is not associated with the kickstart file, registration will not occur in the satellite generated %post section. If one is associated, it will be used for registration.

20.9 downloadRenderedKickstart

Description

Downloads the Cobbler-rendered Kickstart file.

Parameters

- string sessionKey
- string ksLabel - The label of the kickstart to download.

Return Value

- string - The contents of the kickstart file.

20.10 getAdvancedOptions

Description

Get advanced options for a kickstart profile.

Parameters

- string sessionKey
- string ksLabel - Label of kickstart profile to be changed.

Return Value

- array:

    - struct - option

        - string "name"
        - string "arguments"

20.11 getAvailableRepositories

Description

Lists available OS repositories to associate with the provided kickstart profile.

Parameters

- string sessionKey
- string ksLabel

Return Value

> * array:
>
>> * string - repositoryLabel

20.12 getCfgPreservation

Description

> Get ks.cfg preservation option for a kickstart profile.

Parameters

> * string sessionKey
> * string kslabel - Label of kickstart profile to be changed.

Return Value

> * boolean - The value of the option. True means that ks.cfg will be copied to /root, false means that it will not.

20.13 getChildChannels

Description

> Get the child channels for a kickstart profile.

Parameters

> * string sessionKey
> * string kslabel - Label of kickstart profile.

Return Value

- array:

    - string - channelLabel

20.14 getCustomOptions

Description

Get custom options for a kickstart profile.

Parameters

- string sessionKey
- string ksLabel

Return Value

- array:

    - struct - option

        - int "id"
        - string "arguments"

20.15 getKickstartTree

Description

Get the kickstart tree for a kickstart profile.

Parameters

- string sessionKey
- string kslabel - Label of kickstart profile to be changed.

Return Value

- string kstreeLabel - Label of the kickstart tree.

20.16 getRepositories

Description

Lists all OS repositories associated with provided kickstart profile.

Parameters

- string sessionKey
- string ksLabel

Return Value

- array:

    - string - repositoryLabel

20.17 getUpdateType

Description

Get the update type for a kickstart profile.

Parameters

- string sessionKey
- string kslabel - Label of kickstart profile.

Return Value

- string update_type - Update type for this Kickstart Profile.

20.18 getVariables

Description

Returns a list of variables associated with the specified kickstart profile

Parameters

- string sessionKey
- string ksLabel

Return Value

- struct - kickstart variable

    - string "key"
    - string or int "value"

20.19 getVirtualizationType

Description

For given kickstart profile label returns label of virtualization type it's using

Parameters

- string sessionKey
- string ksLabel

Return Value

- string virtLabel - Label of virtualization type.

20.20 listIpRanges

Description

List all ip ranges for a kickstart profile.

Parameters

- string sessionKey
- string label - The label of the kickstart

Return Value

- array:

    - struct - Kickstart Ip Range

- string "ksLabel" - The kickstart label associated with the ip range
- string "max" - The max ip of the range
- string "min" - The min ip of the range

20.21 listScripts

Description

List the pre and post scripts for a kickstart profile in the order they will run during the kickstart.

Parameters

- string sessionKey
- string ksLabel - The label of the kickstart

Return Value

- array:

  - struct - kickstart script

    - int "id"
    - string "name"
    - string "contents"
    - string "script_type" - Which type of script ('pre' or 'post').
    - string "interpreter" - The scripting language interpreter to use for this script. An empty string indicates the default kickstart shell.
    - boolean "chroot" - True if the script will be executed within the chroot environment.
    - boolean "erroronfail" - True if the script will throw an error if it fails.

- boolean "template" - True if templating using cobbler is enabled
- boolean "beforeRegistration" - True if script will run before the server registers and performs server actions.

20.22 orderScripts

Description

Change the order that kickstart scripts will run for this kickstart profile. Scripts will run in the order they appear in the array. There are three arrays, one for all pre scripts, one for the post scripts that run before registration and server actions happen, and one for post scripts that run after registration and server actions. All scripts must be included in one of these lists, as appropriate.

Parameters

- string sessionKey
- string ksLabel - The label of the kickstart
- array:

  - int - IDs of the ordered pre scripts

- array:

  - int - IDs of the ordered post scripts that will run before registration

- array:

  - int - IDs of the ordered post scripts that will run after registration

Return Value

- int - 1 on success, exception thrown otherwise.

20.23 removeIpRange

Description

Remove an ip range from a kickstart profile.

Parameters

- string sessionKey
- string ksLabel - The kickstart label of the ip range you want to remove
- string ip_address - An Ip Address that falls within the range that you are wanting to remove. The min or max of the range will work.

Return Value

- int - 1 on successful removal, 0 if range wasn't found for the specified kickstart, exception otherwise.

20.24 removeScript

Description

Remove a script from a kickstart profile.

Parameters

- string sessionKey
- string ksLabel - The kickstart from which to remove the script from.
- int scriptId - The id of the script to remove.

Return Value

- int - 1 on success, exception thrown otherwise.

20.25 setAdvancedOptions

Description

Set advanced options for a kickstart profile. If 'md5_crypt_rootpw' is set to 'True', 'root_pw' is taken as plaintext and will md5 encrypted on server side, otherwise a hash encoded password (according to the auth option) is expected

Parameters

- string sessionKey
- string ksLabel
- array:

    - struct - advanced options

        - string "name" - Name of the advanced option. Valid Option names: autostep, interactive, install, upgrade, text, network, cdrom, harddrive, nfs, url, lang, langsupport keyboard, mouse, device, deviceprobe, zerombr, clearpart, bootloader, timezone, auth, rootpw, selinux, reboot, firewall, xconfig, skipx, key, ignoredisk, autopart, cmdline, firstboot, graphical, iscsi, iscsiname, logging, monitor, multipath, poweroff, halt, services, shutdown, user, vnc, zfcp, driverdisk, md5_crypt_rootpw
        - string "arguments" - Arguments of the option

Return Value

- int - 1 on success, exception thrown otherwise.

20.26 setCfgPreservation

Description

Set ks.cfg preservation option for a kickstart profile.

Parameters

- string sessionKey
- string kslabel - Label of kickstart profile to be changed.
- boolean preserve - whether or not ks.cfg and all %include fragments will be copied to /root.

Return Value

- int - 1 on success, exception thrown otherwise.

20.27 setChildChannels

Description

Set the child channels for a kickstart profile.

Parameters

- string sessionKey
- string kslabel - Label of kickstart profile to be changed.
- string[] channelLabels - List of labels of child channels

Return Value

- int - 1 on success, exception thrown otherwise.

20.28 setCustomOptions

Description

Set custom options for a kickstart profile.

Parameters

- string sessionKey
- string ksLabel
- string[] options

Return Value

- int - 1 on success, exception thrown otherwise.

20.29 setKickstartTree

Description

Set the kickstart tree for a kickstart profile.

Parameters

- string sessionKey
- string kslabel - Label of kickstart profile to be changed.
- string kstreeLabel - Label of new kickstart tree.

Return Value

- int - 1 on success, exception thrown otherwise.

20.30 setLogging

Description

Set logging options for a kickstart profile.

Parameters

- string sessionKey
- string kslabel - Label of kickstart profile to be changed.
- boolean pre - whether or not to log the pre section of a kickstart to /root/ks-pre.log
- boolean post - whether or not to log the post section of a kickstart to /root/ks-post.log

Return Value

- int - 1 on success, exception thrown otherwise.

20.31 setRepositories

Description

$call.doc

Parameters

- string sessionKey
- string ksLabel
- array:

    - string - repositoryLabel

Return Value

- int - 1 on success, exception thrown otherwise.

20.32 setUpdateType

Description

Set the update typefor a kickstart profile.

Parameters

- string sessionKey
- string kslabel - Label of kickstart profile to be changed.
- string updateType - The new update type to set. Possible values are 'all' and 'none'.

Return Value

- int - 1 on success, exception thrown otherwise.

20.33 setVariables

Description

Associates list of kickstart variables with the specified kickstart profile

Parameters

- string sessionKey
- string ksLabel
- struct - kickstart variable

- string "key"
- string or int "value"

Return Value

- int - 1 on success, exception thrown otherwise.

20.34 setVirtualizationType

Description

For given kickstart profile label sets its virtualization type.

Parameters

- string sessionKey
- string ksLabel
- string typeLabel - One of the following: 'none', 'qemu', 'para_host', 'xenpv', 'xenfv'

Return Value

- int - 1 on success, exception thrown otherwise.

21 kickstart.profile.keys

Provides methods to access and modify the list of activation keys associated with a kickstart profile.

21.1 addActivationKey

Description

Add an activation key association to the kickstart profile

Parameters

- string sessionKey
- string ksLabel - the kickstart profile label
- string key - the activation key

Return Value

- int - 1 on success, exception thrown otherwise.

21.2 getActivationKeys

Description

Lookup the activation keys associated with the kickstart profile.

Parameters

- string sessionKey
- string ksLabel - the kickstart profile label

Return Value

- array:
    - struct - activation key
        - string "key"
        - string "description"

- int "usage_limit"
- string "base_channel_label"
- array "child_channel_labels"

    - string - childChannelLabel
- array "entitlements"

    - string - entitlementLabel
- array "server_group_ids"

    - string - serverGroupId
- array "package_names"

    - string - packageName - (deprecated by packages)
- array "packages"

    - struct - package

        - string "name" - packageName
        - string "arch" - archLabel - optional
- boolean "universal_default"
- boolean "disabled"
- string "contact_method" - One of the following:
    - default
    - ssh-push
    - ssh-push-tunnel

21.3   removeActivationKey

Description

Remove an activation key association from the kickstart profile

Parameters

- string sessionKey
- string ksLabel - the kickstart profile label
- string key - the activation key

Return Value

- int - 1 on success, exception thrown otherwise.

22 kickstart.profile.software

Provides methods to access and modify the software list associated with a kickstart profile.

22.1 appendToSoftwareList

Description

Append the list of software packages to a kickstart profile. Duplicate packages will be ignored.

Parameters

- string sessionKey
- string ksLabel - The label of a kickstart profile.
- string[] packageList - A list of package names to be added to the profile.

Return Value

- int - 1 on success, exception thrown otherwise.

22.2 getSoftwareDetails

Description

Gets kickstart profile software details.

Parameters

- string sessionKey
- string ksLabel - Label of the kickstart profile

Return Value

- struct - Kickstart packages info

- string "noBase" - Install @Base package group
- string "ignoreMissing" - Ignore missing packages

22.3 getSoftwareList

Description

Get a list of a kickstart profile's software packages.

Parameters

- string sessionKey
- string ksLabel - The label of a kickstart profile.

Return Value

- string[] - Get a list of a kickstart profile's software packages.

22.4 setSoftwareDetails

Description

Sets kickstart profile software details.

Parameters

- string sessionKey
- string ksLabel - Label of the kickstart profile
- struct - Kickstart packages info

    - string "noBase" - Install @Base package group
    - string "ignoreMissing" - Ignore missing packages

Return Value

- int - 1 on success, exception thrown otherwise.

22.5 setSoftwareList

Description

Set the list of software packages for a kickstart profile.

Parameters

- string sessionKey
- string ksLabel - The label of a kickstart profile.
- string[] packageList - A list of package names to be set on the profile.

Return Value

- int - 1 on success, exception thrown otherwise.

22.6 setSoftwareList

Description

Set the list of software packages for a kickstart profile.

Parameters

- string sessionKey
- string ksLabel - The label of a kickstart profile.
- string[] packageList - A list of package names to be set on the profile.
- boolean ignoremissing - Ignore missing packages if true
- boolean nobase - Don't install @Base package group if true

Return Value

- int - 1 on success, exception thrown otherwise.

23 kickstart.profile.system

Provides methods to set various properties of a kickstart profile.

23.1 addFilePreservations

Description

Adds the given list of file preservations to the specified kickstart profile.

Parameters

- string sessionKey
- string kickstartLabel
- array:

    - string - filePreservations

Return Value

- int - 1 on success, exception thrown otherwise.

23.2 addKeys

Description

Adds the given list of keys to the specified kickstart profile.

Parameters

- string sessionKey
- string kickstartLabel
- array:

    - string - keyDescription

Return Value

- int - 1 on success, exception thrown otherwise.

23.3 checkConfigManagement

Description

Check the configuration management status for a kickstart profile.

Parameters

- string sessionKey
- string ksLabel - the kickstart profile label

Return Value

- boolean enabled - true if configuration management is enabled; otherwise, false

23.4 checkRemoteCommands

Description

Check the remote commands status flag for a kickstart profile.

Parameters

- string sessionKey
- string ksLabel - the kickstart profile label

Return Value

- boolean enabled - true if remote commands support is enabled; otherwise, false

23.5 disableConfigManagement

Description

Disables the configuration management flag in a kickstart profile so that a system created using this profile will be NOT be configuration capable.

Parameters

- string sessionKey
- string ksLabel - the kickstart profile label

Return Value

- int - 1 on success, exception thrown otherwise.

23.6 disableRemoteCommands

Description

Disables the remote command flag in a kickstart profile so that a system created using this profile will be capable of running remote commands

Parameters

- string sessionKey
- string ksLabel - the kickstart profile label

Return Value

- int - 1 on success, exception thrown otherwise.

23.7 enableConfigManagement

Description

Enables the configuration management flag in a kickstart profile so that a system created using this profile will be configuration capable.

Parameters

- string sessionKey
- string ksLabel - the kickstart profile label

Return Value

- int - 1 on success, exception thrown otherwise.

23.8 enableRemoteCommands

Description

Enables the remote command flag in a kickstart profile so that a system created using this profile will be capable of running remote commands

Parameters

- string sessionKey
- string ksLabel - the kickstart profile label

Return Value

- int - 1 on success, exception thrown otherwise.

23.9 getLocale

Description

Retrieves the locale for a kickstart profile.

Parameters

- string sessionKey
- string ksLabel - the kickstart profile label

Return Value

- struct - locale info

    - string "locale"
    - boolean "useUtc"
        - true - the hardware clock uses UTC
        - false - the hardware clock does not use UTC

23.10 getPartitioningScheme

Description

Get the partitioning scheme for a kickstart profile.

Parameters

- string sessionKey
- string ksLabel - The label of a kickstart profile.

Return Value

- string[] - A list of partitioning commands used to setup the partitions, logical volumes and volume groups."

23.11 getRegistrationType

Description

returns the registration type of a given kickstart profile. Registration Type can be one of reactivation/deletion/none These types determine the behaviour of the registration when using this profile for reprovisioning.

Parameters

- string sessionKey
- string kickstartLabel

Return Value

- string registrationType
  - reactivation
  - deletion
  - none

23.12 getSELinux

Description

Retrieves the SELinux enforcing mode property of a kickstart profile.

Parameters

- string sessionKey
- string ksLabel - the kickstart profile label

Return Value

- string enforcingMode
  - enforcing
  - permissive
  - disabled

23.13 listFilePreservations

Description

Returns the set of all file preservations associated with the given kickstart profile.

Parameters

- string sessionKey
- string kickstartLabel

Return Value

- array:

    - struct - file list

        - string "name"
        - array "file_names"

            - string - name

23.14 listKeys

Description

Returns the set of all keys associated with the given kickstart profile.

Parameters

- string sessionKey
- string kickstartLabel

Return Value

- array:

    - struct - key

        - string "description"
        - string "type"
        - string "content"

23.15 removeFilePreservations

Description

Removes the given list of file preservations from the specified kickstart profile.

Parameters

- string sessionKey
- string kickstartLabel
- array:
    - string - filePreservations

Return Value

- int - 1 on success, exception thrown otherwise.

23.16 removeKeys

Description

Removes the given list of keys from the specified kickstart profile.

Parameters

- string sessionKey
- string kickstartLabel
- array:
    - string - keyDescription

Return Value

- int - 1 on success, exception thrown otherwise.

23.17 setLocale

Description

Sets the locale for a kickstart profile.

Parameters

- string sessionKey
- string ksLabel - the kickstart profile label

- string locale - the locale
- boolean useUtc
  - true - the hardware clock uses UTC
  - false - the hardware clock does not use UTC

Return Value

- int - 1 on success, exception thrown otherwise.

23.18   setPartitioningScheme

Description

Set the partitioning scheme for a kickstart profile.

Parameters

- string sessionKey
- string ksLabel - The label of the kickstart profile to update.
- string[] scheme - The partitioning scheme is a list of partitioning command strings used to setup the partitions, volume groups and logical volumes.

Return Value

- int - 1 on success, exception thrown otherwise.

23.19   setRegistrationType

Description

Sets the registration type of a given kickstart profile. Registration Type can be one of reactivation/deletion/none These types determine the behaviour of the re registration when using this profile.

Parameters

- string sessionKey
- string kickstartLabel

- string registrationType
    - reactivation - to try and generate a reactivation key and use that to register the system when reprovisioning a system.
        - deletion - to try and delete the existing system profile and reregister the system being reprovisioned as new
        - none - to preserve the status quo and leave the current system as a duplicate on a reprovision.

Return Value

- int - 1 on success, exception thrown otherwise.

23.20 setSELinux

Description

Sets the SELinux enforcing mode property of a kickstart profile so that a system created using this profile will be have the appropriate SELinux enforcing mode.

Parameters

- string sessionKey
- string ksLabel - the kickstart profile label
- string enforcingMode - the selinux enforcing mode
    - enforcing
        - permissive
        - disabled

Return Value

- int - 1 on success, exception thrown otherwise.

24 kickstart.snippet

Provides methods to create kickstart files

24.1 createOrUpdate

Description

Will create a snippet with the given name and contents if it doesn't exist. If it does exist, the existing snippet will be updated.

Parameters

- string sessionKey
- string name
- string contents

Return Value

- struct - snippet

  - string "name"
  - string "contents"
  - string "fragment" - The string to include in a kickstart file that will generate this snippet.
  - string "file" - The local path to the file containing this snippet.

24.2 delete

Description

Delete the specified snippet. If the snippet is not found, 0 is returned.

Parameters

- string sessionKey
- string name

Return Value

- int - 1 on success, exception thrown otherwise.

24.3 listAll

Description

List all cobbler snippets for the logged in user

Parameters

- string sessionKey

Return Value

- array:

  - struct - snippet

    - string "name"
    - string "contents"
    - string "fragment" - The string to include in a kickstart file that will generate this snippet.
    - string "file" - The local path to the file containing this snippet.

24.4 listCustom

Description

List only custom snippets for the logged in user. These snipppets are editable.

Parameters

- string sessionKey

Return Value

- array:

  - struct - snippet

- string "name"
- string "contents"
- string "fragment" - The string to include in a kickstart file that will generate this snippet.
- string "file" - The local path to the file containing this snippet.

24.5 listDefault

Description

List only pre-made default snippets for the logged in user. These snipppets are not editable.

Parameters

- string sessionKey

Return Value

- array:

  - struct - snippet

    - string "name"
    - string "contents"
    - string "fragment" - The string to include in a kickstart file that will generate this snippet.
    - string "file" - The local path to the file containing this snippet.

25 kickstart.tree

Provides methods to access and modify the kickstart trees.

25.1 create

Description

Create a Kickstart Tree (Distribution) in Satellite.

Parameters

- string sessionKey
- string treeLabel - The new kickstart tree label.
- string basePath - Path to the base or root of the kickstart tree.
- string channelLabel - Label of channel to associate with the kickstart tree.
- string installType - Label for KickstartInstallType (rhel_2.1, rhel_3, rhel_4, rhel_5, fedora_9).

Return Value

- int - 1 on success, exception thrown otherwise.

25.2 delete

Description

Delete a Kickstart Tree (Distribution) in Satellite.

Parameters

- string sessionKey
- string treeLabel - Label for the kickstart tree to delete.

Return Value

- int - 1 on success, exception thrown otherwise.

25.3 deleteTreeAndProfiles

Description

Delete a kickstarttree and any profiles associated with this kickstart tree. WARNING: This will delete all profiles associated with this kickstart tree!

Parameters

- string sessionKey
- string treeLabel - Label for the kickstart tree to delete.

Return Value

- int - 1 on success, exception thrown otherwise.

25.4 getDetails

Description

The detailed information about a kickstartable tree given the tree name.

Parameters

- string sessionKey
- string treeLabel - Label of kickstartable tree to search.

Return Value

- struct - kickstartable tree

  - int "id"
  - string "label"
  - string "abs_path"
  - int "channel_id"
  - struct - kickstart install type

- int "id"
- string "label"
- string "name"

25.5 list

Description

List the available kickstartable trees for the given channel.

Parameters

- string sessionKey
- string channelLabel - Label of channel to search.

Return Value

- array:

    - struct - kickstartable tree

        - int "id"
        - string "label"
        - string "base_path"
        - int "channel_id"

25.6 listInstallTypes

Description

List the available kickstartable install types (rhel2,3,4,5 and fedora9+).

Parameters

- string sessionKey

Return Value

- array:

    - struct - kickstart install type

- int "id"
- string "label"
- string "name"

25.7 rename

Description

Rename a Kickstart Tree (Distribution) in Satellite.

Parameters

- string sessionKey
- string originalLabel - Label for the kickstart tree to rename.
- string newLabel - The kickstart tree's new label.

Return Value

- int - 1 on success, exception thrown otherwise.

25.8 update

Description

Edit a Kickstart Tree (Distribution) in Satellite.

Parameters

- string sessionKey
- string treeLabel - Label for the kickstart tree.
- string basePath - Path to the base or root of the kickstart tree.
- string channelLabel - Label of channel to associate with kickstart tree.
- string installType - Label for KickstartInstallType (rhel_2.1, rhel_3, rhel_4, rhel_5, fedora_9).

Return Value

- int - 1 on success, exception thrown otherwise.

26 org

Contains methods to access common organization management functions available from the web interface.

26.1 create

Description

Create a new organization and associated administrator account.

Parameters

- string sessionKey
- string orgName - Organization name. Must meet same criteria as in the web UI.
- string adminLogin - New administrator login name.
- string adminPassword - New administrator password.
- string prefix - New administrator's prefix. Must match one of the values available in the web UI. (i.e. Dr., Mr., Mrs., Sr., etc.)
- string firstName - New administrator's first name.
- string lastName - New administrator's first name.
- string email - New administrator's e-mail.
- boolean usePamAuth - True if PAM authentication should be used for the new administrator account.

Return Value

- struct - organization info

    - int "id"
    - string "name"
    - int "active_users" - Number of active users in the organization.
    - int "systems" - Number of systems in the organization.
    - int "trusts" - Number of trusted organizations.
    - int "system_groups" - Number of system groups in the organization. (optional)
    - int "activation_keys" - Number of activation keys in the organization. (optional)
    - int "kickstart_profiles" - Number of kickstart profiles in the organization. (optional)

- int "configuration_channels" - Number of configuration channels in the organization. (optional)
- boolean "staging_content_enabled" - Is staging content enabled in organization. (optional)

26.2 delete

Description

Delete an organization. The default organization (i.e. orgId = 1) cannot be deleted.

Parameters

- string sessionKey
- int orgId

Return Value

- int - 1 on success, exception thrown otherwise.

26.3 getCrashFileSizeLimit

Description

Get the organization wide crash file size limit. The limit value must be a non-negative number, zero means no limit.

Parameters

- string sessionKey
- int orgId

Return Value

- int - Crash file size limit.

26.4 getDetails

Description

The detailed information about an organization given the organization ID.

Parameters

- string sessionKey
- int orgId

Return Value

- struct - organization info

  - int "id"
  - string "name"
  - int "active_users" - Number of active users in the organization.
  - int "systems" - Number of systems in the organization.
  - int "trusts" - Number of trusted organizations.
  - int "system_groups" - Number of system groups in the organization. (optional)
  - int "activation_keys" - Number of activation keys in the organization. (optional)
  - int "kickstart_profiles" - Number of kickstart profiles in the organization. (optional)
  - int "configuration_channels" - Number of configuration channels in the organization. (optional)
  - boolean "staging_content_enabled" - Is staging content enabled in organization. (optional)

26.5 getDetails

Description

The detailed information about an organization given the organization name.

Parameters

- string sessionKey
- string name

Return Value

- struct - organization info

  - int "id"
  - string "name"

- int "active_users" - Number of active users in the organization.
- int "systems" - Number of systems in the organization.
- int "trusts" - Number of trusted organizations.
- int "system_groups" - Number of system groups in the organization. (optional)
- int "activation_keys" - Number of activation keys in the organization. (optional)
- int "kickstart_profiles" - Number of kickstart profiles in the organization. (optional)
- int "configuration_channels" - Number of configuration channels in the organization. (optional)
- boolean "staging_content_enabled" - Is staging content enabled in organization. (optional)

26.6 getPolicyForScapFileUpload

Description

Get the status of SCAP detailed result file upload settings for the given organization.

Parameters

- string sessionKey
- int orgId

Return Value

- struct - scap_upload_info

    - boolean "enabled" - Aggregation of detailed SCAP results is enabled.
    - int "size_limit" - Limit (in Bytes) for a single SCAP file upload.

26.7 getPolicyForScapResultDeletion

Description

Get the status of SCAP result deletion settings for the given organization.

Parameters

- string sessionKey
- int orgId

Return Value

- struct - scap_deletion_info

  - boolean "enabled" - Deletion of SCAP results is enabled
  - int "retention_period" - Period (in days) after which a scan can be deleted (if enabled).

26.8 isCrashReportingEnabled

Description

Get the status of crash reporting settings for the given organization. Returns true if enabled, false otherwise.

Parameters

- string sessionKey
- int orgId

Return Value

- boolean - Get the status of crash reporting settings.

26.9 isCrashfileUploadEnabled

Description

Get the status of crash file upload settings for the given organization. Returns true if enabled, false otherwise.

Parameters

- string sessionKey
- int orgId

Return Value

- boolean - Get the status of crash file upload settings.

26.10 isErrataEmailNotifsForOrg

Description

Returns whether errata e-mail notifications are enabled for the organization

Parameters

- string sessionKey
- int orgId

Return Value

- boolean - Returns the status of the errata e-mail notification setting for the organization

26.11 isOrgConfigManagedByOrgAdmin

Description

Returns whether Organization Administrator is able to manage his organization configuration. This organization configuration may have a high impact on the whole Spacewalk/Satellite performance

Parameters

- string sessionKey
- int orgId

Return Value

- boolean - Returns the status org admin management setting

26.12 listOrgs

Description

Returns the list of organizations.

Parameters

- string sessionKey

Return Value

- array:

  - struct - organization info

    - int "id"
    - string "name"
    - int "active_users" - Number of active users in the organization.
    - int "systems" - Number of systems in the organization.
    - int "trusts" - Number of trusted organizations.
    - int "system_groups" - Number of system groups in the organization. (optional)
    - int "activation_keys" - Number of activation keys in the organization. (optional)
    - int "kickstart_profiles" - Number of kickstart profiles in the organization. (optional)

- int "configuration_channels" - Number of configuration channels in the organization. (optional)
- boolean "staging_content_enabled" - Is staging content enabled in organization. (optional)

26.13 listUsers

Description

Returns the list of users in a given organization.

Parameters

- string sessionKey
- int orgId

Return Value

- array:

    - struct - user

        - string "login"
        - string "login_uc"
        - string "name"
        - string "email"
        - boolean "is_org_admin"

26.14 migrateSystems

Description

Migrate systems from one organization to another. If executed by a Satellite administrator, the systems will be migrated from their current organization to the organization specified by the toOrgId. If executed by an organization administrator, the systems must exist in the same organization as that administrator and the systems will be migrated to the organization specified by the toOrgId. In any scenario, the origination and destination organizations must be defined in a trust.

Parameters

- string sessionKey
- int toOrgId - ID of the organization where the system(s) will be migrated to.
- array:

  - int - systemId

Return Value

- array:

  - int - serverIdMigrated

26.15 setCrashFileSizeLimit

Description

Set the organization wide crash file size limit. The limit value must be non-negative, zero means no limit.

Parameters

- string sessionKey
- int orgId
- int limit - The limit to set (non-negative value).

Return Value

- int - 1 on success, exception thrown otherwise.

26.16 setCrashReporting

Description

Set the status of crash reporting settings for the given organization. Disabling crash reporting will automatically disable crash file upload.

Parameters

- string sessionKey
- int orgId
- boolean enable - Use true/false to enable/disable

Return Value

- int - 1 on success, exception thrown otherwise.

26.17 setCrashfileUpload

Description

Set the status of crash file upload settings for the given organization. Modifying the settings is possible as long as crash reporting is enabled.

Parameters

- string sessionKey
- int orgId
- boolean enable - Use true/false to enable/disable

Return Value

- int - 1 on success, exception thrown otherwise.

26.18 setErrataEmailNotifsForOrg

Description

Dis/enables errata e-mail notifications for the organization

Parameters

- string sessionKey
- int orgId
- boolean enable - Use true/false to enable/disable

Return Value

- int - 1 on success, exception thrown otherwise.

26.19 setOrgConfigManagedByOrgAdmin

Description

Sets whether Organization Administrator can manage his organization configuration. This organization configuration may have a high impact on the whole Spacewalk/Satellite performance

Parameters

- string sessionKey
- int orgId
- boolean enable - Use true/false to enable/disable

Return Value

- int - 1 on success, exception thrown otherwise.

26.20 setPolicyForScapFileUpload

Description

Set the status of SCAP detailed result file upload settings for the given organization.

Parameters

- string sessionKey
- int orgId
- struct - scap_upload_info

    - boolean "enabled" - Aggregation of detailed SCAP results is enabled.
    - int "size_limit" - Limit (in Bytes) for a single SCAP file upload.

Return Value

- int - 1 on success, exception thrown otherwise.

26.21 setPolicyForScapResultDeletion

Description

Set the status of SCAP result deletion settins for the given organization.

Parameters

- string sessionKey
- int orgId
- struct - scap_deletion_info

  - boolean "enabled" - Deletion of SCAP results is enabled
  - int "retention_period" - Period (in days) after which a scan can be deleted (if enabled).

Return Value

- int - 1 on success, exception thrown otherwise.

26.22 updateName

Description

Updates the name of an organization

Parameters

- string sessionKey
- int orgId
- string name - Organization name. Must meet same criteria as in the web UI.

Return Value

- struct - organization info

- int "id"
- string "name"
- int "active_users" - Number of active users in the organization.
- int "systems" - Number of systems in the organization.
- int "trusts" - Number of trusted organizations.
- int "system_groups" - Number of system groups in the organization. (optional)
- int "activation_keys" - Number of activation keys in the organization. (optional)
- int "kickstart_profiles" - Number of kickstart profiles in the organization. (optional)
- int "configuration_channels" - Number of configuration channels in the organization. (optional)
- boolean "staging_content_enabled" - Is staging content enabled in organization. (optional)

27 org.trusts

Contains methods to access common organization trust information available from the web interface.

27.1 addTrust

Description

Add an organization to the list of trusted organizations.

Parameters

- string sessionKey
- int orgId
- int trustOrgId

Return Value

- int - 1 on success, exception thrown otherwise.

27.2 getDetails

Description

The trust details about an organization given the organization's ID.

Parameters

- string sessionKey
- int trustOrgId - Id of the trusted organization

Return Value

- struct - org trust details

    - dateTime.iso8601 "created" - Date the organization was created
    - dateTime.iso8601 "trusted_since" - Date the organization was defined as trusted
    - int "channels_provided" - Number of channels provided by the organization.

- int "channels_consumed" - Number of channels consumed by the organization.
- int "systems_migrated_to" - Number of systems migrated to the organization.
- int "systems_migrated_from" - Number of systems migrated from the organization.

27.3 listChannelsConsumed

Description

Lists all software channels that the organization given may consume from the user's organization.

Parameters

- string sessionKey
- int trustOrgId - Id of the trusted organization

Return Value

- array:

  - struct - channel info

    - int "channel_id"
    - string "channel_name"
    - int "packages"
    - int "systems"

27.4 listChannelsProvided

Description

Lists all software channels that the organization given is providing to the user's organization.

Parameters

- string sessionKey
- int trustOrgId - Id of the trusted organization

Return Value

- array:

    - struct - channel info

        - int "channel_id"
        - string "channel_name"
        - int "packages"
        - int "systems"

27.5 listOrgs

Description

List all organanizations trusted by the user's organization.

Parameters

- string sessionKey

Return Value

- array:

    - struct - trusted organizations

        - int "org_id"
        - string "org_name"
        - int "shared_channels"

27.6 listSystemsAffected

Description

Get a list of systems within the trusted organization that would be affected if the trust relationship was removed. This basically lists systems that are sharing at least (1) package.

Parameters

- string sessionKey
- int orgId
- string trustOrgId

Return Value

- array:

    - struct - affected systems

        - int "systemId"
        - string "systemName"

27.7 listTrusts

Description

Returns the list of trusted organizations.

Parameters

- string sessionKey
- int orgId

Return Value

- array:

    - struct - trusted organizations

        - int "orgId"
        - string "orgName"
        - bool "trustEnabled"

27.8 removeTrust

Description

Remove an organization to the list of trusted organizations.

Parameters

- string sessionKey
- int orgId
- int trustOrgId

Return Value

- int - 1 on success, exception thrown otherwise.

28 packages

Methods to retrieve information about the Packages contained within this server.

28.1 findByNvrea

Description

Lookup the details for packages with the given name, version, release, architecture label, and (optionally) epoch.

Parameters

- string sessionKey
- string name
- string version
- string release
- string epoch - If set to something other than empty string, strict matching will be used and the epoch string must be correct. If set to an empty string, if the epoch is null or there is only one NVRA combination, it will be returned. (Empty string is recommended.)
- string archLabel

Return Value

- array:

  - struct - package

    - string "name"
    - string "version"
    - string "release"
    - string "epoch"
    - int "id"
    - string "arch_label"
    - string "path" - The path on that file system that the package resides

- string "provider" - The provider of the package, determined by the gpg key it was signed with.
- dateTime.iso8601 "last_modified"

28.2 getDetails

Description

Retrieve details for the package with the ID.

Parameters

- string sessionKey
- int packageId

Return Value

- struct - package

    - int "id"
    - string "name"
    - string "epoch"
    - string "version"
    - string "release"
    - string "arch_label"
    - array "providing_channels"

        - string - Channel label providing this package.
    - string "build_host"
    - string "description"
    - string "checksum"
    - string "checksum_type"
    - string "vendor"
    - string "summary"
    - string "cookie"
    - string "license"
    - string "file"
    - string "build_date"
    - string "last_modified_date"

- string "size"
- string "path" - The path on the Satellite's file system that the package resides.
- string "payload_size"

28.3 getPackage

Description

Retrieve the package file associated with a package. (Consider using packages.getPackageUrl for larger files.)

Parameters

- string sessionKey
- int package_id

Return Value

- binary object - package file

28.4 getPackageUrl

Description

Retrieve the url that can be used to download a package. This will expire after a certain time period.

Parameters

- string sessionKey
- int package_id

Return Value

- string - the download url

28.5 listChangelog

Description

List the change log for a package.

Parameters

- string sessionKey
- int packageId

Return Value

- string

28.6 listDependencies

Description

List the dependencies for a package.

Parameters

- string sessionKey
- int packageId

Return Value

- array:

    - struct - dependency

        - string "dependency"
        - string "dependency_type" - One of the following:
            - requires
            - conflicts
            - obsoletes
            - provides
            - recommends
            - suggests

- supplements
- enhances
- string "dependency_modifier"

28.7 listFiles

Description

List the files associated with a package.

Parameters

- string sessionKey
- int packageId

Return Value

- array:

    - struct - file info

        - string "path"
        - string "type"
        - string "last_modified_date"
        - string "checksum"
        - string "checksum_type"
        - int "size"
        - string "linkto"

28.8 listProvidingChannels

Description

List the channels that provide the a package.

Parameters

- string sessionKey
- int packageId

Return Value

- array:

    - struct - channel

        - string "label"
        - string "parent_label"
        - string "name"

28.9 listProvidingErrata

Description

List the errata providing the a package.

Parameters

- string sessionKey
- int packageId

Return Value

- array:

    - struct - errata

        - string "advisory"
        - string "issue_date"
        - string "last_modified_date"
        - string "update_date"
        - string "synopsis"
        - string "type"

28.10 listSourcePackages

Description

List all source packages in user's organization.

Parameters

- string sessionKey

Return Value

- array:

    - struct - source_package

        - int "id"
        - string "name"

28.11   removePackage

Description

Remove a package from the satellite.

Parameters

- string sessionKey
- int packageId

Return Value

- int - 1 on success, exception thrown otherwise.

28.12   removeSourcePackage

Description

Remove a source package.

Parameters

- string sessionKey
- int packageSourceId

Return Value

- int - 1 on success, exception thrown otherwise.

29 packages.provider

Methods to retrieve information about Package Providers associated with packages.

29.1 associateKey

Description

Associate a package security key and with the package provider. If the provider or key doesn't exist, it is created. User executing the request must be a Satellite administrator.

Parameters

- string sessionKey
- string providerName - The provider name
- string key - The actual key
- string type - The type of the key. Currently, only 'gpg' is supported

Return Value

- int - 1 on success, exception thrown otherwise.

29.2 list

Description

List all Package Providers. User executing the request must be a Satellite administrator.

Parameters

- string sessionKey

Return Value

- array:
  - struct - package provider
    - string "name"
    - array "keys"

- struct - package security key

  - string "key"
  - string "type"

29.3 listKeys

Description

List all security keys associated with a package provider. User executing the request must be a Satellite administrator.

Parameters

- string sessionKey
- string providerName - The provider name

Return Value

- array:

  - struct - package security key

    - string "key"
    - string "type"

30 packages.search

Methods to interface to package search capabilities in search server..

30.1 advanced

Description

Advanced method to search lucene indexes with a passed in query written in Lucene Query Parser syntax.

Lucene Query Parser syntax is defined at lucene.apache.org.

Fields searchable for Packages: name, epoch, version, release, arch, description, summary

Lucene Query Example: "name:kernel AND version:2.6.18 AND -description:devel"

Parameters

- string sessionKey
- string luceneQuery - a query written in the form of Lucene QueryParser Syntax

Return Value

- array:

  - struct - package overview

    - int "id"
    - string "name"
    - string "summary"
    - string "description"
    - string "version"
    - string "release"
    - string "arch"

- string "epoch"
- string "provider"

30.2 advancedWithActKey

Description

Advanced method to search lucene indexes with a passed in query written in Lucene Query Parser syntax, additionally this method will limit results to those which are associated with a given activation key.

Lucene Query Parser syntax is defined at lucene.apache.org.

Fields searchable for Packages: name, epoch, version, release, arch, description, summary

Lucene Query Example: "name:kernel AND version:2.6.18 AND -description:devel"

Parameters

- string sessionKey
- string luceneQuery - a query written in the form of Lucene QueryParser Syntax
- string actKey - activation key to look for packages in

Return Value

- array:

  - struct - package overview

    - int "id"
    - string "name"
    - string "summary"
    - string "description"
    - string "version"
    - string "release"
    - string "arch"

- string "epoch"
- string "provider"

30.3 advancedWithChannel

Description

Advanced method to search lucene indexes with a passed in query written in Lucene Query Parser syntax, additionally this method will limit results to those which are in the passed in channel label.

Lucene Query Parser syntax is defined at lucene.apache.org.

Fields searchable for Packages: name, epoch, version, release, arch, description, summary

Lucene Query Example: "name:kernel AND version:2.6.18 AND -description:devel"

Parameters

- string sessionKey
- string luceneQuery - a query written in the form of Lucene QueryParser Syntax
- string channelLabel - Channel Label

Return Value

- array:

  - struct - package overview

    - int "id"
    - string "name"
    - string "summary"
    - string "description"
    - string "version"
    - string "release"
    - string "arch"

- string "epoch"
- string "provider"

30.4 name

Description

Search the lucene package indexes for all packages which match the given name.

Parameters

- string sessionKey
- string name - package name to search for

Return Value

- array:

  - struct - package overview

    - int "id"
    - string "name"
    - string "summary"
    - string "description"
    - string "version"
    - string "release"
    - string "arch"
    - string "epoch"
    - string "provider"

30.5 nameAndDescription

Description

Search the lucene package indexes for all packages which match the given query in name or description

Parameters

- string sessionKey
- string query - text to match in package name or description

Return Value

- array:

    - struct - package overview

        - int "id"
        - string "name"
        - string "summary"
        - string "description"
        - string "version"
        - string "release"
        - string "arch"
        - string "epoch"
        - string "provider"

30.6   nameAndSummary

Description

Search the lucene package indexes for all packages which match the given query in name or summary.

Parameters

- string sessionKey
- string query - text to match in package name or summary

Return Value

- array:

    - struct - package overview

        - int "id"
        - string "name"

- string "summary"
- string "description"
- string "version"
- string "release"
- string "arch"
- string "epoch"
- string "provider"

31 preferences.locale

Provides methods to access and modify user locale information

31.1 listLocales

Description

Returns a list of all understood locales. Can be used as input to setLocale.

Parameters

- None

Return Value

- array:

  - string - Locale code.

31.2 listTimeZones

Description

Returns a list of all understood timezones. Results can be used as input to setTimeZone.

Parameters

- None

Return Value

- array:

  - struct - timezone

- int "time_zone_id" - Unique identifier for timezone.
- string "olson_name" - Name as identified by the Olson database.

31.3 setLocale

Description

Set a user's locale.

Parameters

- string sessionKey
- string login - User's login name.
- string locale - Locale to set. (from listLocales)

Return Value

- int - 1 on success, exception thrown otherwise.

31.4 setTimeZone

Description

Set a user's timezone.

Parameters

- string sessionKey
- string login - User's login name.
- int tzid - Timezone ID. (from listTimeZones)

Return Value

- int - 1 on success, exception thrown otherwise.

32 proxy

Provides methods to activate/deactivate a proxy server.

32.1 activateProxy

Description

Activates the proxy identified by the given client certificate i.e. systemid file.

Parameters

- string systemid - systemid file
- string version - Version of proxy to be registered.

Return Value

- int - 1 on success, exception thrown otherwise.

32.2 createMonitoringScout

Description

Create Monitoring Scout for proxy.
Available since: 10.7

Parameters

- string systemid - systemid file

Return Value

- string

32.3 deactivateProxy

Description

Deactivates the proxy identified by the given client certificate i.e. systemid file.

Parameters

- string systemid - systemid file

Return Value

- int - 1 on success, exception thrown otherwise.

32.4 isProxy

Description

Test, if the system identified by the given client certificate i.e. systemid file, is proxy.

Parameters

- string systemid - systemid file

Return Value

- int - 1 on success, exception thrown otherwise.

32.5 listAvailableProxyChannels

Description

List available version of proxy channel for system identified by the given client certificate i.e. systemid file.

Available since: 10.5

Parameters

- string systemid - systemid file

Return Value

- array:

  - string - version

33 satellite

Provides methods to obtain details on the Satellite.

33.1 isMonitoringEnabled

Description

Indicates if monitoring is enabled on the satellite

Parameters

- string sessionKey

Return Value

- boolean True if monitoring is enabled

33.2 isMonitoringEnabledBySystemId

Description

Indicates if monitoring is enabled on the satellite

Parameters

- string systemid - systemid file

Return Value

- boolean True if monitoring is enabled

33.3 listProxies

Description

List the proxies within the user's organization.

Parameters

- string sessionKey

Return Value

- array:

  - struct - system

    - int "id"
    - string "name"
    - dateTime.iso8601 "last_checkin" - Last time server successfully checked in
    - dateTime.iso8601 "created" - Server registration time
    - dateTime.iso8601 "last_boot" - Last server boot time
    - int "extra_pkg_count" - Number of packages not belonging to any assigned channel
    - int "outdated_pkg_count" - Number of out-of-date packages

34 schedule

Methods to retrieve information about scheduled actions.

34.1 archiveActions

Description

Archive all actions in the given list.

Parameters

- string sessionKey
- array:

    - int - action id

Return Value

- int - 1 on success, exception thrown otherwise.

34.2 cancelActions

Description

Cancel all actions in given list. If an invalid action is provided, none of the actions given will canceled.

Parameters

- string sessionKey
- array:

    - int - action id

Return Value

- int - 1 on success, exception thrown otherwise.

34.3 deleteActions

Description

Delete all archived actions in the given list.

Parameters

- string sessionKey
- array:

    - int - action id

Return Value

- int - 1 on success, exception thrown otherwise.

34.4 failSystemAction

Description

Fail specific event on specified system

Parameters

- string sessionKey
- int serverId
- int actionId

Return Value

- int - 1 on success, exception thrown otherwise.

34.5 failSystemAction

Description

Fail specific event on specified system

Parameters

- string sessionKey
- int serverId
- int actionId
- string message

Return Value

- int - 1 on success, exception thrown otherwise.

34.6 listAllActions

Description

Returns a list of all actions. This includes completed, in progress, failed and archived actions.

Parameters

- string sessionKey

Return Value

- array:

  - struct - action

    - int "id" - Action Id.
    - string "name" - Action name.

- string "type" - Action type.
- string "scheduler" - The user that scheduled the action. (optional)
- dateTime.iso8601 "earliest" - The earliest date and time the action will be performed
- int "completedSystems" - Number of systems that completed the action.
- int "failedSystems" - Number of systems that failed the action.
- int "inProgressSystems" - Number of systems that are in progress.

34.7 listArchivedActions

Description

Returns a list of actions that have been archived.

Parameters

- string sessionKey

Return Value

- array:

    - struct - action

        - int "id" - Action Id.
        - string "name" - Action name.
        - string "type" - Action type.
        - string "scheduler" - The user that scheduled the action. (optional)
        - dateTime.iso8601 "earliest" - The earliest date and time the action will be performed
        - int "completedSystems" - Number of systems that completed the action.
        - int "failedSystems" - Number of systems that failed the action.
        - int "inProgressSystems" - Number of systems that are in progress.

34.8 listCompletedActions

Description

Returns a list of actions that have completed successfully.

Parameters

- string sessionKey

Return Value

- array:

  - struct - action

    - int "id" - Action Id.
    - string "name" - Action name.
    - string "type" - Action type.
    - string "scheduler" - The user that scheduled the action. (optional)
    - dateTime.iso8601 "earliest" - The earliest date and time the action will be performed
    - int "completedSystems" - Number of systems that completed the action.
    - int "failedSystems" - Number of systems that failed the action.
    - int "inProgressSystems" - Number of systems that are in progress.

34.9 listCompletedSystems

Description

Returns a list of systems that have completed a specific action.

Parameters

- string sessionKey
- string actionId

Return Value

- array:

  - struct - system

    - int "server_id"
    - string "server_name" - Server name.
    - string "base_channel" - Base channel used by the server.

- dateTime.iso8601 "timestamp" - The time the action was completed
- string "message" - Optional message containing details on the execution of the action. For example, if the action failed, this will contain the failure text.

34.10 listFailedActions

Description

Returns a list of actions that have failed.

Parameters

- string sessionKey

Return Value

- array:

  - struct - action

    - int "id" - Action Id.
    - string "name" - Action name.
    - string "type" - Action type.
    - string "scheduler" - The user that scheduled the action. (optional)
    - dateTime.iso8601 "earliest" - The earliest date and time the action will be performed
    - int "completedSystems" - Number of systems that completed the action.
    - int "failedSystems" - Number of systems that failed the action.
    - int "inProgressSystems" - Number of systems that are in progress.

34.11 listFailedSystems

Description

Returns a list of systems that have failed a specific action.

Parameters

- string sessionKey
- string actionId

Return Value

- array:

  - struct - system

    - int "server_id"
    - string "server_name" - Server name.
    - string "base_channel" - Base channel used by the server.
    - dateTime.iso8601 "timestamp" - The time the action was completed
    - string "message" - Optional message containing details on the execution of the action. For example, if the action failed, this will contain the failure text.

34.12 listInProgressActions

Description

Returns a list of actions that are in progress.

Parameters

- string sessionKey

Return Value

- array:

  - struct - action

    - int "id" - Action Id.
    - string "name" - Action name.
    - string "type" - Action type.
    - string "scheduler" - The user that scheduled the action. (optional)
    - dateTime.iso8601 "earliest" - The earliest date and time the action will be performed

- int "completedSystems" - Number of systems that completed the action.
- int "failedSystems" - Number of systems that failed the action.
- int "inProgressSystems" - Number of systems that are in progress.

34.13 listInProgressSystems

Description

Returns a list of systems that have a specific action in progress.

Parameters

- string sessionKey
- string actionId

Return Value

- array:

    - struct - system

        - int "server_id"
        - string "server_name" - Server name.
        - string "base_channel" - Base channel used by the server.
        - dateTime.iso8601 "timestamp" - The time the action was completed
        - string "message" - Optional message containing details on the execution of the action. For example, if the action failed, this will contain the failure text.

34.14 rescheduleActions

Description

Reschedule all actions in the given list.

Parameters

- string sessionKey
- array:

  - int - action id
- boolean onlyFailed - True to only reschedule failed actions, False to reschedule all

Return Value

- int - 1 on success, exception thrown otherwise.

35 subscriptionmatching.pinnedsubscription

Provides the namespace for operations on Pinned Subscriptions

35.1 create

Description

Creates a Pinned Subscription based on given subscription and system

Parameters

- string sessionKey - Session token, issued at login
- int subscriptionId - Subscription Id
- int systemId - System Id

Return Value

- struct - pinned subscription

  - int "id"
  - int "subscription_id"
  - int "system_id"

35.2 delete

Description

Deletes Pinned Subscription with given id

Parameters

- string sessionKey - Session token, issued at login
- int pinnedSubscriptionId - Pinned Subscription id

Return Value

- int - 1 on success, exception thrown otherwise.

35.3 list

Description

Lists all PinnedSubscriptions

Parameters

- string sessionKey - Session token, issued at login

Return Value

- array:

    - struct - pinned subscription

        - int "id"
        - int "subscription_id"
        - int "system_id"

36 sync.content

Provides the namespace for the content synchronization methods.

36.1 addChannel

Description

> Add a new channel to the SUSE Manager database

Parameters

- string sessionKey - Session token, issued at login
- string channelLabel - Label of the channel to add
- string mirrorUrl - Sync from mirror temporarily

Return Value

- int - 1 on success, exception thrown otherwise.

36.2 addCredentials

Description

> Add organization credentials (mirror credentials) to SUSE Manager.

Parameters

- string sessionKey - Session token, issued at login
- string username - Organization credentials (Mirror credentials) username
- string password - Organization credentials (Mirror credentials) password
- boolean primary - Make this the primary credentials

Return Value

- int - 1 on success, exception thrown otherwise.

36.3 deleteCredentials

Description

Delete organization credentials (mirror credentials) from SUSE Manager.

Parameters

- string sessionKey - Session token, issued at login
- string username - Username of credentials to delete

Return Value

- int - 1 on success, exception thrown otherwise.

36.4 listChannels

Description

List all accessible channels.

Parameters

- string sessionKey - Session token, issued at login

Return Value

- array:
  - struct - channel
    - string "arch" - Architecture of the channel
    - string "description" - Description of the channel
    - string "family" - Channel family label
    - boolean "is_signed" - Channel has signed metadata

- string "label" - Label of the channel
- string "name" - Name of the channel
- boolean "optional" - Channel is optional
- string "parent" - The label of the parent channel
- string "product_name" - Product name
- string "product_version" - Product version
- string "source_url" - Repository source URL
- string "status" - Status: available, unavailable or installed
- string "summary" - Channel summary
- string "update_tag" - Update tag

36.5 listCredentials

Description

List organization credentials (mirror credentials) available in SUSE Manager.

Parameters

- string sessionKey - Session token, issued at login

Return Value

- array:

  - struct - credentials

    - int "id" - ID of the credentials
    - string "user" - username
    - boolean "isPrimary" - primary

36.6 listProducts

Description

List all accessible products.

Parameters

- string sessionKey - Session token, issued at login

Return Value

- array:

    - struct - product

        - string "friendly_name" - Friendly name of the product
        - string "arch" - Architecture
        - string "status" - 'available', 'unavailable' or 'installed'
        - array:

            - struct - channel

                - string "arch" - Architecture of the channel
                - string "description" - Description of the channel
                - string "family" - Channel family label
                - boolean "is_signed" - Channel has signed metadata
                - string "label" - Label of the channel
                - string "name" - Name of the channel
                - boolean "optional" - Channel is optional
                - string "parent" - The label of the parent channel
                - string "product_name" - Product name
                - string "product_version" - Product version
                - string "source_url" - Repository source URL
                - string "status" - Status: available, unavailable or installed
                - string "summary" - Channel summary
                - string "update_tag" - Update tag

        - array:

            - struct - extension product

                - string "friendly_name" - Friendly name of extension product
                - string "arch" - Architecture

- string "status" - 'available', 'unavailable' or 'installed'
- array:

  - struct - channel

    - string "arch" - Architecture of the channel
    - string "description" - Description of the channel
    - string "family" - Channel family label
    - boolean "is_signed" - Channel has signed metadata
    - string "label" - Label of the channel
    - string "name" - Name of the channel
    - boolean "optional" - Channel is optional
    - string "parent" - The label of the parent channel
    - string "product_name" - Product name
    - string "product_version" - Product version
    - string "source_url" - Repository source URL
    - string "status" - Status: available, unavailable or installed
    - string "summary" - Channel summary
    - string "update_tag" - Update tag

36.7 synchronizeChannelFamilies

Description

Synchronize channel families between the Customer Center and the SUSE Manager database.

Parameters

- string sessionKey - Session token, issued at login

Return Value

- int - 1 on success, exception thrown otherwise.

36.8 synchronizeChannels

Description

Synchronize channels between the Customer Center and the SUSE Manager database.

Parameters

- string sessionKey - Session token, issued at login
- string mirrorUrl - Sync from mirror temporarily

Return Value

- int - 1 on success, exception thrown otherwise.

36.9 synchronizeProductChannels

Description

Synchronize SUSE product channels between the Customer Center and the SUSE Manager database.

Parameters

- string sessionKey - Session token, issued at login

Return Value

- int - 1 on success, exception thrown otherwise.

36.10 synchronizeProducts

Description

Synchronize SUSE products between the Customer Center and the SUSE Manager database.

Parameters

- string sessionKey - Session token, issued at login

Return Value

- int - 1 on success, exception thrown otherwise.

36.11 synchronizeSubscriptions

Description

Synchronize subscriptions between the Customer Center and the SUSE Manager database.

Parameters

- string sessionKey - Session token, issued at login

Return Value

- int - 1 on success, exception thrown otherwise.

37   sync.master

Contains methods to set up information about known-"masters", for use on the "slave" side of ISS

37.1   addToMaster

Description

Add a single organizations to the list of those the specified Master has exported to this Slave

Parameters

- string sessionKey
- int id - Id of the desired Master
- struct - master-org details

    - int "masterOrgId"
    - string "masterOrgName"
    - int "localOrgId"

Return Value

- int - 1 on success, exception thrown otherwise.

37.2   create

Description

Create a new Master, known to this Slave.

Parameters

- string sessionKey
- string label - Master's fully-qualified domain name

Return Value

- struct - IssMaster info

- int "id"
- string "label"
- string "caCert"
- boolean "isCurrentMaster"

37.3 delete

Description

Remove the specified Master

Parameters

- string sessionKey
- int id - Id of the Master to remove

Return Value

- int - 1 on success, exception thrown otherwise.

37.4 getDefaultMaster

Description

Return the current default-Master for this Slave

Parameters

- string sessionKey

Return Value

- struct - IssMaster info
  - int "id"
  - string "label"

- string "caCert"
- boolean "isCurrentMaster"

37.5 getMaster

Description

>   Find a Master by specifying its ID

Parameters

- string sessionKey
- int id - Id of the desired Master

Return Value

- struct - IssMaster info

    - int "id"
    - string "label"
    - string "caCert"
    - boolean "isCurrentMaster"

37.6 getMasterByLabel

Description

>   Find a Master by specifying its label

Parameters

- string sessionKey
- string label - Label of the desired Master

Return Value

- struct - IssMaster info

    - int "id"
    - string "label"

- string "caCert"
- boolean "isCurrentMaster"

37.7 getMasterOrgs

Description

List all organizations the specified Master has exported to this Slave

Parameters

- string sessionKey
- int id - Id of the desired Master

Return Value

- array:

  - struct - IssMasterOrg info

    - int "masterOrgId"
    - string "masterOrgName"
    - int "localOrgId"

37.8 getMasters

Description

Get all the Masters this Slave knows about

Parameters

- string sessionKey

Return Value

- array:

  - struct - IssMaster info

    - int "id"
    - string "label"

- string "caCert"
- boolean "isCurrentMaster"

37.9 hasMaster

Description

> Check if this host is reading configuration from an ISS master.

Parameters

- None

Return Value

- boolean - True if has an ISS master, false otherwise.

37.10 makeDefault

Description

> Make the specified Master the default for this Slave's satellite-sync

Parameters

- string sessionKey
- int id - Id of the Master to make the default

Return Value

- int - 1 on success, exception thrown otherwise.

37.11 mapToLocal

Description

> Add a single organizations to the list of those the specified Master has exported to this Slave

Parameters

- string sessionKey
- int masterId - Id of the desired Master

- int masterOrgId - Id of the desired Master
- int localOrgId - Id of the desired Master

Return Value

- int - 1 on success, exception thrown otherwise.

37.12 setCaCert

Description

Set the CA-CERT filename for specified Master on this Slave

Parameters

- string sessionKey
- int id - Id of the Master to affect
- string caCertFilename - path to specified Master's CA cert

Return Value

- int - 1 on success, exception thrown otherwise.

37.13 setMasterOrgs

Description

Reset all organizations the specified Master has exported to this Slave

Parameters

- string sessionKey
- int id - Id of the desired Master
- array:
    - struct - master-org details

- int "masterOrgId"
- string "masterOrgName"
- int "localOrgId"

Return Value

- int - 1 on success, exception thrown otherwise.

37.14 unsetDefaultMaster

Description

Make this slave have no default Master for satellite-sync

Parameters

- string sessionKey

Return Value

- int - 1 on success, exception thrown otherwise.

37.15 update

Description

Updates the label of the specified Master

Parameters

- string sessionKey
- int id - Id of the Master to update
- string label - Desired new label

Return Value

- struct - IssMaster info

    - int "id"
    - string "label"

- string "caCert"
- boolean "isCurrentMaster"

38 sync.slave

Contains methods to set up information about allowed-"slaves", for use on the "master" side of ISS

38.1 create

Description

Create a new Slave, known to this Master.

Parameters

- string sessionKey
- string slave - Slave's fully-qualified domain name
- boolean enabled - Let this slave talk to us?
- boolean allowAllOrgs - Export all our orgs to this slave?

Return Value

- struct - IssSlave info

    - int "id"
    - string "slave"
    - boolean "enabled"
    - boolean "allowAllOrgs"

38.2 delete

Description

Remove the specified Slave

Parameters

- string sessionKey
- int id - Id of the Slave to remove

Return Value

- int - 1 on success, exception thrown otherwise.

38.3 getAllowedOrgs

Description

Get all orgs this Master is willing to export to the specified Slave

Parameters

- string sessionKey
- int id - Id of the desired Slave

Return Value

- array:

  - int - ids of allowed organizations

38.4 getSlave

Description

Find a Slave by specifying its ID

Parameters

- string sessionKey
- int id - Id of the desired Slave

Return Value

- struct - IssSlave info

  - int "id"
  - string "slave"

- boolean "enabled"
- boolean "allowAllOrgs"

38.5 getSlaveByName

Description

Find a Slave by specifying its Fully-Qualified Domain Name

Parameters

- string sessionKey
- string fqdn - Domain-name of the desired Slave

Return Value

- struct - IssSlave info

  - int "id"
  - string "slave"
  - boolean "enabled"
  - boolean "allowAllOrgs"

38.6 getSlaves

Description

Get all the Slaves this Master knows about

Parameters

- string sessionKey

Return Value

- array:

  - struct - IssSlave info

    - int "id"
    - string "slave"

- boolean "enabled"
- boolean "allowAllOrgs"

38.7 setAllowedOrgs

Description

Set the orgs this Master is willing to export to the specified Slave

Parameters

- string sessionKey
- int id - Id of the desired Slave
- array:
    - int - List of org-ids we're willing to export

Return Value

- int - 1 on success, exception thrown otherwise.

38.8 update

Description

Updates attributes of the specified Slave

Parameters

- string sessionKey
- int id - Id of the Slave to update
- string slave - Slave's fully-qualified domain name
- boolean enabled - Let this slave talk to us?
- boolean allowAllOrgs - Export all our orgs to this Slave?

Return Value

- struct - IssSlave info
    - int "id"
    - string "slave"

- boolean "enabled"
- boolean "allowAllOrgs"

39 system

Provides methods to access and modify registered system.

39.1 addEntitlements

Description

    Add entitlements to a server. Entitlements a server already has are quietly ignored.

Parameters

- string sessionKey
- int serverId
- array:

    - string - entitlementLabel - one of following: virtualization_host, enterprise_entitled

Return Value

- int - 1 on success, exception thrown otherwise.

39.2 addNote

Description

    Add a new note to the given server.

Parameters

- string sessionKey
- int serverId
- string subject - What the note is about.
- string body - Content of the note.

Return Value

- int - 1 on success, exception thrown otherwise.

39.3 applyErrata

Description

Schedules an action to apply errata updates to a system.

Deprecated - being replaced by system.scheduleApplyErrata(string sessionKey, int serverId, array[int errataId])

Parameters

- string sessionKey
- int serverId
- array:

    - int - errataId

Return Value

- int - 1 on success, exception thrown otherwise.

39.4 bootstrap

Description

Bootstrap a system for management via either Salt or Salt SSH.

Parameters

- string sessionKey
- string host - Hostname or IP address of target
- int sshPort - SSH port on target machine
- string sshUser - SSH user on target machine
- string sshPassword - SSH password of given user
- string activationKey - Activation key
- boolean saltSSH - Manage system with Salt SSH

Return Value

- int - 1 on success, exception thrown otherwise.

39.5 bootstrap

Description

Bootstrap a system for management via either Salt or Salt SSH.

Parameters

- string sessionKey
- string host - Hostname or IP address of target
- int sshPort - SSH port on target machine
- string sshUser - SSH user on target machine
- string sshPassword - SSH password of given user
- string activationKey - Activation key
- int proxyId - System ID of proxy to use
- boolean saltSSH - Manage system with Salt SSH

Return Value

- int - 1 on success, exception thrown otherwise.

39.6 comparePackageProfile

Description

Compare a system's packages against a package profile. In the result returned, 'this_system' represents the server provided as an input and 'other_system' represents the profile provided as an input.

Parameters

- string sessionKey
- int serverId
- string profileLabel

Return Value

- array:

  - struct - Package Metadata

    - int "package_name_id"
    - string "package_name"
    - string "package_epoch"
    - string "package_version"
    - string "package_release"
    - string "package_arch"
    - string "this_system" - Version of package on this system.
    - string "other_system" - Version of package on the other system.
    - int "comparison"
      - 0 - No difference.
      - 1 - Package on this system only.
      - 2 - Newer package version on this system.
      - 3 - Package on other system only.
      - 4 - Newer package version on other system.

39.7 comparePackages

Description

Compares the packages installed on two systems.

Parameters

- string sessionKey
- int thisServerId
- int otherServerId

Return Value

- array:

  - struct - Package Metadata

- int "package_name_id"
- string "package_name"
- string "package_epoch"
- string "package_version"
- string "package_release"
- string "package_arch"
- string "this_system" - Version of package on this system.
- string "other_system" - Version of package on the other system.
- int "comparison"
  - 0 - No difference.
  - 1 - Package on this system only.
  - 2 - Newer package version on this system.
  - 3 - Package on other system only.
  - 4 - Newer package version on other system.

39.8 createPackageProfile

Description

Create a new stored Package Profile from a systems installed package list.

Parameters

- string sessionKey
- int serverId
- string profileLabel
- string description

Return Value

- int - 1 on success, exception thrown otherwise.

39.9 createSystemRecord

Description

Creates a cobbler system record with the specified kickstart label

Parameters

- string sessionKey
- int serverId
- string ksLabel

Return Value

- int - 1 on success, exception thrown otherwise.

39.10 createSystemRecord

Description

Creates a cobbler system record for a system that is not registered.

Parameters

- string sessionKey
- string sysName
- string ksLabel
- string kOptions
- string comment
- array:
  - struct - network device
    - string "name"
    - string "mac"
    - string "ip"

Return Value

- int - 1 on success, exception thrown otherwise.

39.11 deleteCustomValues

Description

Delete the custom values defined for the custom system information keys provided from the given system.

(Note: Attempt to delete values of non-existing keys throws exception. Attempt to delete value of existing key which has assigned no values doesn't throw exception.)

Parameters

- string sessionKey
- int serverId
- array:

    - string - customInfoLabel

Return Value

- int - 1 on success, exception thrown otherwise.

39.12 deleteGuestProfiles

Description

Delete the specified list of guest profiles for a given host

Parameters

- string sessionKey
- int hostId
- array:

    - string - guestNames

Return Value

- int - 1 on success, exception thrown otherwise.

39.13 deleteNote

Description

Deletes the given note from the server.

Parameters

- string sessionKey
- int serverId
- int noteId

Return Value

- int - 1 on success, exception thrown otherwise.

39.14 deleteNotes

Description

Deletes all notes from the server.

Parameters

- string sessionKey
- int serverId

Return Value

- int - 1 on success, exception thrown otherwise.

39.15 deletePackageProfile

Description

Delete a package profile

Parameters

- string sessionKey
- int profileId

Return Value

- int - 1 on success, exception thrown otherwise.

39.16 deleteSystem

Description

Delete a system given its client certificate.
Available since: 10.10

Parameters

- string systemid - systemid file

Return Value

- int - 1 on success, exception thrown otherwise.

39.17 deleteSystem

Description

Delete a system given its server id synchronously

Parameters

- string sessionKey
- int serverId

Return Value

- int - 1 on success, exception thrown otherwise.

39.18 deleteSystems

Description

Delete systems given a list of system ids asynchronously.

Parameters

- string sessionKey
- array:

  - int - serverId

Return Value

- int - 1 on success, exception thrown otherwise.

39.19 deleteTagFromSnapshot

Description

Deletes tag from system snapshot

Parameters

- string sessionKey
- int serverId
- string tagName

Return Value

- int - 1 on success, exception thrown otherwise.

39.20 downloadSystemId

Description

Get the system ID file for a given server.

Parameters

- string sessionKey
- int serverId

Return Value

- string

39.21 getConnectionPath

Description

Get the list of proxies that the given system connects through in order to reach the server.

Parameters

- string sessionKey
- int serverId

Return Value

- array:

  - struct - proxy connection path details

    - int "position" - Position of proxy in chain. The proxy that the system connects directly to is listed in position 1.
    - int "id" - Proxy system id
    - string "hostname" - Proxy host name

39.22 getCpu

Description

Gets the CPU information of a system.

Parameters

- string sessionKey
- int serverId

Return Value

- struct - CPU

- string "cache"
- string "family"
- string "mhz"
- string "flags"
- string "model"
- string "vendor"
- string "arch"
- string "stepping"
- string "count"
- int "socket_count (if available)"

39.23 getCustomValues

Description

Get the custom data values defined for the server.

Parameters

- string sessionKey
- int serverId

Return Value

- struct - custom value

  - string "custom info label"

39.24 getDetails

Description

Get system details.

Parameters

- string sessionKey
- int serverId

Return Value

- struct - server details

  - int "id" - System id
  - string "profile_name"
  - string "base_entitlement" - System's base entitlement label
  - array "string"

    - addon_entitlements - System's addon entitlements labels, currently only 'virtualization_host'
  - boolean "auto_update" - True if system has auto errata updates enabled.
  - string "release" - The Operating System release (i.e. 4AS, 5Server
  - string "address1"
  - string "address2"
  - string "city"
  - string "state"
  - string "country"
  - string "building"
  - string "room"
  - string "rack"
  - string "description"
  - string "hostname"
  - dateTime.iso8601 "last_boot"
  - string "osa_status" - Either 'unknown', 'offline', or 'online'.
  - boolean "lock_status" - True indicates that the system is locked. False indicates that the system is unlocked.
  - string "virtualization" - Virtualization type - for virtual guests only (optional)

- string "contact_method" - One of the following:
  - default
  - ssh-push
  - ssh-push-tunnel

39.25 getDevices

Description

Gets a list of devices for a system.

Parameters

- string sessionKey
- int serverId

Return Value

- array:

  - struct - device

    - string "device" - optional
    - string "device_class" - Includes CDROM, FIREWIRE, HD, USB, VIDEO, OTHER, etc.
    - string "driver"
    - string "description"
    - string "bus"
    - string "pcitype"

39.26 getDmi

Description

Gets the DMI information of a system.

Parameters

- string sessionKey
- int serverId

Return Value

- struct - DMI

  - string "vendor"
  - string "system"
  - string "product"
  - string "asset"
  - string "board"
  - string "bios_release" - (optional)
  - string "bios_vendor" - (optional)
  - string "bios_version" - (optional)

39.27 getEntitlements

Description

Gets the entitlements for a given server.

Parameters

- string sessionKey
- int serverId

Return Value

- array:

  - string - entitlement_label

39.28 getEventHistory

Description

Returns a list history items associated with the system, ordered from newest to oldest. Note that the details may be empty for events that were scheduled against the system (as compared to instant). For more information on such events, see the system.listSystemEvents operation.

Parameters

- string sessionKey
- int serverId

Return Value

- array:

    - struct - History Event

        - dateTime.iso8601 "completed" - Date that the event occurred (optional)
        - string "summary" - Summary of the event
        - string "details" - Details of the event

39.29 getId

Description

Get system IDs and last check in information for the given system name.

Parameters

- string sessionKey
- string systemName

Return Value

- array:

    - struct - system

        - int "id"
        - string "name"
        - dateTime.iso8601 "last_checkin" - Last time server successfully checked in
        - dateTime.iso8601 "created" - Server registration time
        - dateTime.iso8601 "last_boot" - Last server boot time

- int "extra_pkg_count" - Number of packages not belonging to any assigned channel
- int "outdated_pkg_count" - Number of out-of-date packages

39.30 getInstalledProducts

Description

Get a list of installed products for given system

Parameters

- User loggedInUser
- int serverId

Return Value

- array:

  - struct - installed product

    - string "name"
    - boolean "isBaseProduct"
    - string "version" - returned only if applies
    - string "arch" - returned only if applies
    - string "release" - returned only if applies
    - string "friendlyName" - returned only if available

39.31 getKernelLivePatch

Description

Returns the currently active kernel live patching version relative to the running kernel version of the system, or empty string if live patching feature is not in use for the given system.

Parameters

- string sessionKey
- int serverId

Return Value

- string

39.32 getMemory

Description

Gets the memory information for a system.

Parameters

- string sessionKey
- int serverId

Return Value

- struct - memory

    - int "ram" - The amount of physical memory in MB.
    - int "swap" - The amount of swap space in MB.

39.33 getName

Description

Get system name and last check in information for the given system ID.

Parameters

- string sessionKey
- string serverId

Return Value

- struct - name info

- int "id" - Server id
- string "name" - Server name
- dateTime.iso8601 "last_checkin" - Last time server successfully checked in

39.34 getNetwork

Description

Get the addresses and hostname for a given server.

Parameters

- string sessionKey
- int serverId

Return Value

- struct - network info

    - string "ip" - IPv4 address of server
    - string "ip6" - IPv6 address of server
    - string "hostname" - Hostname of server

39.35 getNetworkDevices

Description

Returns the network devices for the given server.

Parameters

- string sessionKey
- int serverId

Return Value

- array:

    - struct - network device

- string "ip" - IP address assigned to this network device
- string "interface" - Network interface assigned to device e.g. eth0
- string "netmask" - Network mask assigned to device
- string "hardware_address" - Hardware Address of device.
- string "module" - Network driver used for this device.
- string "broadcast" - Broadcast address for device.
- array "ipv6" - List of IPv6 addresses
- array:

  - struct - ipv6 address

    - string "address" - IPv6 address of this network device
    - string "netmask" - IPv6 netmask of this network device
    - string "scope" - IPv6 address scope

39.36 getOsaPing

Description

get details about a ping sent to a system using OSA

Parameters

- User loggedInUser
- int serverId

Return Value

- struct - osaPing

- String "state" - state of the system (unknown, online, offline)
- dateTime.iso8601 "lastMessageTime" - time of the last received response (1970/01/01 00:00:00 if never received a response)
- dateTime.iso8601 "lastPingTime" - time of the last sent ping (1970/01/01 00:00:00 if no ping is pending)

39.37 getRegistrationDate

Description

Returns·the date the system was registered.

Parameters

- string sessionKey
- int serverId

Return Value

- dateTime.iso8601 - The date the system was registered, in local time.

39.38 getRelevantErrata

Description

Returns a list of all errata that are relevant to the system.

Parameters

- string sessionKey
- int serverId

Return Value

- array:
    - struct - errata
        - int "id" - Errata ID.
        - string "date" - Date erratum was created.
        - string "update_date" - Date erratum was updated.

- string "advisory_synopsis" - Summary of the erratum.
- string "advisory_type" - Type label such as Security, Bug Fix
- string "advisory_name" - Name such as RHSA, etc

39.39 getRelevantErrataByType

Description

Returns a list of all errata of the specified type that are relevant to the system.

Parameters

- string sessionKey
- int serverId
- string advisoryType - type of advisory (one of of the following: 'Security Advisory', 'Product Enhancement Advisory', 'Bug Fix Advisory'

Return Value

- array:

    - struct - errata

        - int "id" - Errata ID.
        - string "date" - Date erratum was created.
        - string "update_date" - Date erratum was updated.
        - string "advisory_synopsis" - Summary of the erratum.
        - string "advisory_type" - Type label such as Security, Bug Fix
        - string "advisory_name" - Name such as RHSA, etc

39.40 getRunningKernel

Description

Returns the running kernel of the given system.

Parameters

- string sessionKey
- int serverId

Return Value

- string

39.41 getScriptActionDetails

Description

Returns script details for script run actions

Parameters

- string sessionKey
- int actionId - ID of the script run action.

Return Value

- struct - Script details

  - int "id" - action id
  - string "content" - script content
  - string "run_as_user" - Run as user
  - string "run_as_group" - Run as group
  - int "timeout" - Timeout in seconds
  - array:

    - struct - script result

      - int "serverId" - ID of the server the script runs on.
      - dateTime.iso8601 "startDate" - Time script began execution.
      - dateTime.iso8601 "stopDate" - Time script stopped execution.
      - int "returnCode" - Script execution return code.

- string "output" - Output of the script (base64 encoded according to the output_enc64 attribute)
  - boolean "output_enc64" - Identifies base64 encoded output

39.42 getScriptResults

Description

Fetch results from a script execution. Returns an empty array if no results are yet available.

Parameters

- string sessionKey
- int actionId - ID of the script run action.

Return Value

- array:

  - struct - script result

    - int "serverId" - ID of the server the script runs on.
    - dateTime.iso8601 "startDate" - Time script began execution.
    - dateTime.iso8601 "stopDate" - Time script stopped execution.
    - int "returnCode" - Script execution return code.
    - string "output" - Output of the script (base64 encoded according to the output_enc64 attribute)
    - boolean "output_enc64" - Identifies base64 encoded output

39.43 getSubscribedBaseChannel

Description

Provides the base channel of a given system

Parameters

- string sessionKey
- int serverId

Return Value

- struct - channel

    - int "id"
    - string "name"
    - string "label"
    - string "arch_name"
    - string "arch_label"
    - string "summary"
    - string "description"
    - string "checksum_label"
    - dateTime.iso8601 "last_modified"
    - string "maintainer_name"
    - string "maintainer_email"
    - string "maintainer_phone"
    - string "support_policy"
    - string "gpg_key_url"
    - string "gpg_key_id"
    - string "gpg_key_fp"
    - dateTime.iso8601 "yumrepo_last_sync" - (optional)
    - string "end_of_life"
    - string "parent_channel_label"
    - string "clone_original"
    - array:

        - struct - contentSources

            - int "id"
            - string "label"
            - string "sourceUrl"
            - string "type"

39.44 getSystemCurrencyMultipliers

Description

Get the System Currency score multipliers

Parameters

- string sessionKey

Return Value

- Map of score multipliers

39.45 getSystemCurrencyScores

Description

Get the System Currency scores for all servers the user has access to

Parameters

- string sessionKey

Return Value

- array:

  - struct - system currency

    - int "sid"
    - int "critical security errata count"
    - int "important security errata count"
    - int "moderate security errata count"
    - int "low security errata count"
    - int "bug fix errata count"
    - int "enhancement errata count"
    - int "system currency score"

39.46 getUnscheduledErrata

Description

Provides an array of errata that are applicable to a given system.

Parameters

- string sessionKey
- int serverId

Return Value

- array:

    - struct - errata

        - int "id" - Errata Id
        - string "date" - Date erratum was created.
        - string "advisory_type" - Type of the advisory.
        - string "advisory_name" - Name of the advisory.
        - string "advisory_synopsis" - Summary of the erratum.

39.47 getUuid

Description

Get the UUID from the given system ID.

Parameters

- string sessionKey
- int serverId

Return Value

- string

39.48 getVariables

Description

Lists kickstart variables set in the system record for the specified server. Note: This call assumes that a system record exists in cobbler for the given system and will raise an XMLRPC fault if that is not the case. To create a system record over xmlrpc use system.createSystemRecord To create a system record in the Web UI please go to System -> <Specified System> -> Provisioning -> Select a Kickstart profile -> Create Cobbler System Record.

Parameters

- string sessionKey
- int serverId

Return Value

- struct - System kickstart variables

    - boolean "netboot" - netboot enabled
    - array "kickstart variables"

        - struct - kickstart variable

            - string "key"
            - string or int "value"

39.49 isNvreInstalled

Description

Check if the package with the given NVRE is installed on given system.

Parameters

- string sessionKey
- int serverId
- string name - Package name.
- string version - Package version.
- string release - Package release.

Return Value

- 1 if package exists, 0 if not, exception is thrown if an error occurs

39.50 isNvreInstalled

Description

Is the package with the given NVRE installed on given system.

Parameters

- string sessionKey
- int serverId
- string name - Package name.
- string version - Package version.
- string release - Package release.
- string epoch - Package epoch.

Return Value

- 1 if package exists, 0 if not, exception is thrown if an error occurs

39.51 listActivationKeys

Description

List the activation keys the system was registered with. An empty list will be returned if an activation key was not used during registration.

Parameters

- string sessionKey
- int serverId

Return Value

- array:
    - string - key

39.52 listActiveSystems

Description

Returns a list of active servers visible to the user.

Parameters

- string sessionKey

Return Value

- array:

    - struct - system

        - int "id"
        - string "name"
        - dateTime.iso8601 "last_checkin" - Last time server successfully checked in
        - dateTime.iso8601 "created" - Server registration time
        - dateTime.iso8601 "last_boot" - Last server boot time
        - int "extra_pkg_count" - Number of packages not belonging to any assigned channel
        - int "outdated_pkg_count" - Number of out-of-date packages

39.53 listActiveSystemsDetails

Description

Given a list of server ids, returns a list of active servers' details visible to the user.

Parameters

- string sessionKey
- array:

    - int - serverIds

Return Value

- array:

    - struct - server details

        - int "id" - The server's id
        - string "name" - The server's name

- dateTime.iso8601 "last_checkin" - Last time server successfully checked in (in UTC)
- int "ram" - The amount of physical memory in MB.
- int "swap" - The amount of swap space in MB.
- struct "network_devices" - The server's network devices
- struct - network device

    - string "ip" - IP address assigned to this network device
    - string "interface" - Network interface assigned to device e.g. eth0
    - string "netmask" - Network mask assigned to device
    - string "hardware_address" - Hardware Address of device.
    - string "module" - Network driver used for this device.
    - string "broadcast" - Broadcast address for device.
    - array "ipv6" - List of IPv6 addresses
    - array:

        - struct - ipv6 address

            - string "address" - IPv6 address of this network device
            - string "netmask" - IPv6 netmask of this network device
            - string "scope" - IPv6 address scope

- struct "dmi_info" - The server's dmi info
- struct - DMI

    - string "vendor"
    - string "system"
    - string "product"
    - string "asset"
    - string "board"
    - string "bios_release" - (optional)
    - string "bios_vendor" - (optional)
    - string "bios_version" - (optional)

- struct "cpu_info" - The server's cpu info
- struct - CPU

    - string "cache"
    - string "family"
    - string "mhz"

- string "flags"
- string "model"
- string "vendor"
- string "arch"
- string "stepping"
- string "count"
- int "socket_count (if available)"
- array "subscribed_channels" - List of subscribed channels
- array:

  - struct - channel

    - int "channel_id" - The channel id.
    - string "channel_label" - The channel label.
- array "active_guest_system_ids" - List of virtual guest system ids for active guests
- array:

  - int "guest_id" - The guest's system id.

39.54 listAdministrators

Description

Returns a list of users which can administer the system.

Parameters

- string sessionKey
- int serverId

Return Value

- array:

  - struct - user

    - int "id"
    - string "login"

- string "login_uc" - upper case version of the login
- boolean "enabled" - true if user is enabled, false if the user is disabled

39.55 listAllInstallablePackages

Description

Get the list of all installable packages for a given system.

Parameters

- string sessionKey
- int serverId

Return Value

- struct - package

  - string "name"
  - string "version"
  - string "release"
  - string "epoch"
  - int "id"
  - string "arch_label"

39.56 listBaseChannels

Description

Returns a list of subscribable base channels.

Deprecated - being replaced by listSubscribableBaseChannels(string sessionKey, int serverId)

Parameters

- string sessionKey
- int serverId

Return Value

- array:

    - struct - channel

        - int "id" - Base Channel ID.
        - string "name" - Name of channel.
        - string "label" - Label of Channel
        - int "current_base" - 1 indicates it is the current base channel

39.57 listChildChannels

Description

Returns a list of subscribable child channels. This only shows channels the system is *not* currently subscribed to.

Deprecated - being replaced by listSubscribableChildChannels(string sessionKey, int serverId)

Parameters

- string sessionKey
- int serverId

Return Value

- array:

    - struct - child channel

        - int "id"
        - string "name"
        - string "label"
        - string "summary"

- string "has_license"
- string "gpg_key_url"

39.58 listDuplicatesByHostname

Description

List duplicate systems by Hostname.

Parameters

- string sessionKey

Return Value

- array:

  - struct - Duplicate Group

    - string "hostname"
    - array "systems"

      - struct - system

        - int "systemId"
        - string "systemName"
        - dateTime.iso8601 "last_checkin" - Last time server successfully checked in

39.59 listDuplicatesByIp

Description

List duplicate systems by IP Address.

Parameters

- string sessionKey

Return Value

- array:

  - struct - Duplicate Group

    - string "ip"
    - array "systems"

      - struct - system

        - int "systemId"
        - string "systemName"
        - dateTime.iso8601 "last_checkin" - Last time server successfully checked in

39.60 listDuplicatesByMac

Description

List duplicate systems by Mac Address.

Parameters

- string sessionKey

Return Value

- array:

  - struct - Duplicate Group

    - string "mac"
    - array "systems"

      - struct - system

- int "systemId"
- string "systemName"
- dateTime.iso8601 "last_checkin" - Last time server successfully checked in

39.61 listExtraPackages

Description

List extra packages for a system

Parameters

- string sessionKey
- int serverId

Return Value

- array:

    - struct - package

        - string "name"
        - string "version"
        - string "release"
        - string "epoch" - returned only if non-zero
        - string "arch"
        - date "installtime" - returned only if known

39.62 listGroups

Description

List the available groups for a given system.

Parameters

- string sessionKey
- int serverId

Return Value

- array:

  - struct - system group

    - int "id" - server group id
    - int "subscribed" - 1 if the given server is subscribed to this server group, 0 otherwise
    - string "system_group_name" - Name of the server group
    - string "sgid" - server group id (Deprecated)

39.63 listInactiveSystems

Description

Lists systems that have been inactive for the default period of inactivity

Parameters

- string sessionKey

Return Value

- array:

  - struct - system

    - int "id"
    - string "name"
    - dateTime.iso8601 "last_checkin" - Last time server successfully checked in
    - dateTime.iso8601 "created" - Server registration time
    - dateTime.iso8601 "last_boot" - Last server boot time

- int "extra_pkg_count" - Number of packages not belonging to any assigned channel
- int "outdated_pkg_count" - Number of out-of-date packages

39.64 listInactiveSystems

Description

Lists systems that have been inactive for the specified number of days..

Parameters

- string sessionKey
- int days

Return Value

- array:

    - struct - system

        - int "id"
        - string "name"
        - dateTime.iso8601 "last_checkin" - Last time server successfully checked in
        - dateTime.iso8601 "created" - Server registration time
        - dateTime.iso8601 "last_boot" - Last server boot time
        - int "extra_pkg_count" - Number of packages not belonging to any assigned channel
        - int "outdated_pkg_count" - Number of out-of-date packages

39.65 listLatestAvailablePackage

Description

Get the latest available version of a package for each system

Parameters

- string sessionKey
- array:

    - int - serverId
- string packageName

Return Value

- array:

    - struct - system

        - int "id" - server ID
        - string "name" - server name
        - struct "package" - package structure
        - struct - package

            - int "id"
            - string "name"
            - string "version"
            - string "release"
            - string "epoch"
            - string "arch"

39.66 listLatestInstallablePackages

Description

Get the list of latest installable packages for a given system.

Parameters

- string sessionKey
- int serverId

Return Value

- array:

    - struct - package

        - string "name"
        - string "version"
        - string "release"
        - string "epoch"
        - int "id"
        - string "arch_label"

39.67 listLatestUpgradablePackages

Description

Get the list of latest upgradable packages for a given system.

Parameters

- string sessionKey
- int serverId

Return Value

- array:

    - struct - package

        - string "name"
        - string "arch"
        - string "from_version"
        - string "from_release"
        - string "from_epoch"
        - string "to_version"
        - string "to_release"

- string "to_epoch"
- string "to_package_id"

39.68 listMigrationTargets

Description

List possible migration targets for a system

Parameters

- string sessionKey
- int serverId

Return Value

- array:

  - struct - migrationtarget

    - string "ident"
    - string "friendly"

39.69 listNewerInstalledPackages

Description

Given a package name, version, release, and epoch, returns the list of packages installed on the system w/ the same name that are newer.

Parameters

- string sessionKey
- int serverId
- string name - Package name.
- string version - Package version.
- string release - Package release.
- string epoch - Package epoch.

Return Value

- array:

    - struct - package

        - string "name"
        - string "version"
        - string "release"
        - string "epoch"

39.70 listNotes

Description

Provides a list of notes associated with a system.

Parameters

- string sessionKey
- int serverId

Return Value

- array:

    - struct - note details

        - int "id"
        - string "subject" - Subject of the note
        - string "note" - Contents of the note
        - int "system_id" - The id of the system associated with the note

- string "creator" - Creator of the note if exists (optional)
- date "updated" - Date of the last note update

39.71 listOlderInstalledPackages

Description

Given a package name, version, release, and epoch, returns the list of packages installed on the system with the same name that are older.

Parameters

- string sessionKey
- int serverId
- string name - Package name.
- string version - Package version.
- string release - Package release.
- string epoch - Package epoch.

Return Value

- array:

  - struct - package

    - string "name"
    - string "version"
    - string "release"
    - string "epoch"

39.72 listOutOfDateSystems

Description

Returns list of systems needing package updates.

Parameters

- string sessionKey

Return Value

- array:

    - struct - system

        - int "id"
        - string "name"
        - dateTime.iso8601 "last_checkin" - Last time server successfully checked in
        - dateTime.iso8601 "created" - Server registration time
        - dateTime.iso8601 "last_boot" - Last server boot time
        - int "extra_pkg_count" - Number of packages not belonging to any assigned channel
        - int "outdated_pkg_count" - Number of out-of-date packages

39.73 listPackageProfiles

Description

List the package profiles in this organization

Parameters

- string sessionKey

Return Value

- array:

    - struct - package profile

- int "id"
- string "name"
- string "channel"

39.74 listPackages

Description

List the installed packages for a given system. The attribute installtime is returned since API version 10.10.

Parameters

- string sessionKey
- int serverId

Return Value

- array:

  - struct - package

    - string "name"
    - string "version"
    - string "release"
    - string "epoch"
    - string "arch"
    - date "installtime" - returned only if known

39.75 listPackagesFromChannel

Description

Provides a list of packages installed on a system that are also contained in the given channel. The installed package list did not include arch information before RHEL 5, so it is arch unaware. RHEL 5 systems do upload the arch information, and thus are arch aware.

Parameters

- string sessionKey
- int serverId
- string channelLabel

Return Value

- array:

    - struct - package

        - string "name"
        - string "version"
        - string "release"
        - string "epoch"
        - int "id"
        - string "arch_label"
        - string "path" - The path on that file system that the package resides
        - string "provider" - The provider of the package, determined by the gpg key it was signed with.
        - dateTime.iso8601 "last_modified"

39.76 listPhysicalSystems

Description

Returns a list of all Physical servers visible to the user.

Parameters

- string sessionKey

Return Value

- array:

    - struct - system

        - int "id"
        - string "name"

- dateTime.iso8601 "last_checkin" - Last time server successfully checked in
- dateTime.iso8601 "created" - Server registration time
- dateTime.iso8601 "last_boot" - Last server boot time
- int "extra_pkg_count" - Number of packages not belonging to any assigned channel
- int "outdated_pkg_count" - Number of out-of-date packages

39.77 listSubscribableBaseChannels

Description

Returns a list of subscribable base channels.

Parameters

- string sessionKey
- int serverId

Return Value

- array:

  - struct - channel

    - int "id" - Base Channel ID.
    - string "name" - Name of channel.
    - string "label" - Label of Channel
    - int "current_base" - 1 indicates it is the current base channel

39.78 listSubscribableChildChannels

Description

Returns a list of subscribable child channels. This only shows channels the system is *not* currently subscribed to.

Parameters

- string sessionKey
- int serverId

Return Value

- array:

  - struct - child channel

    - int "id"
    - string "name"
    - string "label"
    - string "summary"
    - string "has_license"
    - string "gpg_key_url"

39.79 listSubscribedChildChannels

Description

Returns a list of subscribed child channels.

Parameters

- string sessionKey
- int serverId

Return Value

- array:

  - struct - channel

    - int "id"
    - string "name"
    - string "label"
    - string "arch_name"
    - string "arch_label"
    - string "summary"
    - string "description"
    - string "checksum_label"
    - dateTime.iso8601 "last_modified"

- string "maintainer_name"
- string "maintainer_email"
- string "maintainer_phone"
- string "support_policy"
- string "gpg_key_url"
- string "gpg_key_id"
- string "gpg_key_fp"
- dateTime.iso8601 "yumrepo_last_sync" - (optional)
- string "end_of_life"
- string "parent_channel_label"
- string "clone_original"
- array:

  - struct - contentSources

    - int "id"
    - string "label"
    - string "sourceUrl"
    - string "type"

39.80 listSuggestedReboot

Description

List systems that require reboot.

Parameters

- string sessionKey

Return Value

- array:

  - struct - system

- int "id"
- string "name"

39.81 listSystemEvents

Description

List system events of the specified type for given server. "actionType" should be exactly the string returned in the action_type field from the listSystemEvents(sessionKey, serverId) method. For example, 'Package Install' or 'Initiate a kickstart for a virtual guest.'
Available since: 10.8

Parameters

- string sessionKey
- int serverId - ID of system.
- string actionType - Type of the action.

Return Value

- array:

  - struct - action

    - int "failed_count" - Number of times action failed.
    - string "modified" - Date modified. (Deprecated by modified_date)
    - dateTime.iso8601 "modified_date" - Date modified.
    - string "created" - Date created. (Deprecated by created_date)
    - dateTime.iso8601 "created_date" - Date created.
    - string "action_type"
    - int "successful_count" - Number of times action was successful.
    - string "earliest_action" - Earliest date this action will occur.
    - int "archived" - If this action is archived. (1 or 0)
    - string "scheduler_user" - available only if concrete user has scheduled the action
    - string "prerequisite" - Pre-requisite action. (optional)
    - string "name" - Name of this action.
    - int "id" - Id of this action.

- string "version" - Version of action.
- string "completion_time" - The date/time the event was completed. Format - > YYYY-MM-dd hh:mm:ss.ms Eg - > 2007-06-04 13:58:13.0. (optional) (Deprecated by completed_date)
- dateTime.iso8601 "completed_date" - The date/time the event was completed. (optional)
- string "pickup_time" - The date/time the action was picked up. Format - > YYYY-MM-dd hh:mm:ss.ms Eg - > 2007-06-04 13:58:13.0. (optional) (Deprecated by pickup_date)
- dateTime.iso8601 "pickup_date" - The date/time the action was picked up. (optional)
- string "result_msg" - The result string after the action executes at the client machine. (optional)
- array "additional_info" - This array contains additional information for the event, if available.

    - struct - info

        - string "detail" - The detail provided depends on the specific event. For example, for a package event, this will be the package name, for an errata event, this will be the advisory name and synopsis, for a config file event, this will be path and optional revision information...etc.
        - string "result" - The result (if included) depends on the specific event. For example, for a package or errata event, no result is included, for a config file event, the result might include an error (if one occurred, such as the file was missing) or in the case of a config file comparison it might include the differenes found.

39.82 listSystemEvents

Description

List all system events for given server. This includes *all* events for the server since it was registered. This may require the caller to filter the results to fetch the specific events they are looking for.

Available since: 10.8

Parameters

- string sessionKey
- int serverId - ID of system.

Return Value

- array:

  - struct - action

    - int "failed_count" - Number of times action failed.
    - string "modified" - Date modified. (Deprecated by modified_date)
    - dateTime.iso8601 "modified_date" - Date modified.
    - string "created" - Date created. (Deprecated by created_date)
    - dateTime.iso8601 "created_date" - Date created.
    - string "action_type"
    - int "successful_count" - Number of times action was successful.
    - string "earliest_action" - Earliest date this action will occur.
    - int "archived" - If this action is archived. (1 or 0)
    - string "scheduler_user" - available only if concrete user has scheduled the action
    - string "prerequisite" - Pre-requisite action. (optional)
    - string "name" - Name of this action.
    - int "id" - Id of this action.
    - string "version" - Version of action.
    - string "completion_time" - The date/time the event was completed. Format - > YYYY-MM-dd hh:mm:ss.ms Eg - > 2007-06-04 13:58:13.0. (optional) (Deprecated by completed_date)
    - dateTime.iso8601 "completed_date" - The date/time the event was completed. (optional)
    - string "pickup_time" - The date/time the action was picked up. Format - > YYYY-MM-dd hh:mm:ss.ms Eg - > 2007-06-04 13:58:13.0. (optional) (Deprecated by pickup_date)
    - dateTime.iso8601 "pickup_date" - The date/time the action was picked up. (optional)

- string "result_msg" - The result string after the action executes at the client machine. (optional)
- array "additional_info" - This array contains additional information for the event, if available.

  - struct - info

    - string "detail" - The detail provided depends on the specific event. For example, for a package event, this will be the package name, for an errata event, this will be the advisory name and synopsis, for a config file event, this will be path and optional revision information...etc.
    - string "result" - The result (if included) depends on the specific event. For example, for a package or errata event, no result is included, for a config file event, the result might include an error (if one occurred, such as the file was missing) or in the case of a config file comparison it might include the differenes found.

39.83 listSystems

Description

Returns a list of all servers visible to the user.

Parameters

- string sessionKey

Return Value

- array:

  - struct - system

    - int "id"
    - string "name"
    - dateTime.iso8601 "last_checkin" - Last time server successfully checked in
    - dateTime.iso8601 "created" - Server registration time

- dateTime.iso8601 "last_boot" - Last server boot time
- int "extra_pkg_count" - Number of packages not belonging to any assigned channel
- int "outdated_pkg_count" - Number of out-of-date packages

39.84 listSystemsWithExtraPackages

Description

List systems with extra packages

Parameters

- string sessionKey

Return Value

- array:

    - struct - system

        - int "id" - System ID
        - string "name" - System profile name
        - int "extra_pkg_count" - Extra packages count

39.85 listSystemsWithPackage

Description

Lists the systems that have the given installed package

Parameters

- string sessionKey
- int pid - the package id

Return Value

- array:

    - struct - system

- int "id"
- string "name"
- dateTime.iso8601 "last_checkin" - Last time server successfully checked in
- dateTime.iso8601 "created" - Server registration time
- dateTime.iso8601 "last_boot" - Last server boot time
- int "extra_pkg_count" - Number of packages not belonging to any assigned channel
- int "outdated_pkg_count" - Number of out-of-date packages

39.86 listSystemsWithPackage

Description

Lists the systems that have the given installed package

Parameters

- string sessionKey
- string name - the package name
- string version - the package version
- string release - the package release

Return Value

- array:

    - struct - system

        - int "id"
        - string "name"
        - dateTime.iso8601 "last_checkin" - Last time server successfully checked in
        - dateTime.iso8601 "created" - Server registration time
        - dateTime.iso8601 "last_boot" - Last server boot time

- int "extra_pkg_count" - Number of packages not belonging to any assigned channel
- int "outdated_pkg_count" - Number of out-of-date packages

39.87 listUngroupedSystems

Description

List systems that are not associated with any system groups.

Parameters

- string sessionKey

Return Value

- array:

  - struct - system

    - int "id"
    - string "name"
    - dateTime.iso8601 "last_checkin" - Last time server successfully checked in
    - dateTime.iso8601 "created" - Server registration time
    - dateTime.iso8601 "last_boot" - Last server boot time
    - int "extra_pkg_count" - Number of packages not belonging to any assigned channel
    - int "outdated_pkg_count" - Number of out-of-date packages

39.88 listUserSystems

Description

List systems for a given user.

Parameters

- string sessionKey
- string login - User's login name.

Return Value

- array:

  - struct - system

    - int "id"
    - string "name"
    - dateTime.iso8601 "last_checkin" - Last time server successfully checked in
    - dateTime.iso8601 "created" - Server registration time
    - dateTime.iso8601 "last_boot" - Last server boot time
    - int "extra_pkg_count" - Number of packages not belonging to any assigned channel
    - int "outdated_pkg_count" - Number of out-of-date packages

39.89 listUserSystems

Description

List systems for the logged in user.

Parameters

- string sessionKey

Return Value

- array:

  - struct - system

    - int "id"
    - string "name"
    - dateTime.iso8601 "last_checkin" - Last time server successfully checked in
    - dateTime.iso8601 "created" - Server registration time
    - dateTime.iso8601 "last_boot" - Last server boot time

- int "extra_pkg_count" - Number of packages not belonging to any assigned channel
- int "outdated_pkg_count" - Number of out-of-date packages

39.90 listVirtualGuests

Description

Lists the virtual guests for a given virtual host

Parameters

- string sessionKey
- int sid - the virtual host's id

Return Value

- array:

    - struct - virtual system

        - int "id"
        - string "name"
        - string "guest_name" - The virtual guest name as provided by the virtual host
        - dateTime.iso8601 "last_checkin" - Last time server successfully checked in.
        - string "uuid"

39.91 listVirtualHosts

Description

Lists the virtual hosts visible to the user

Parameters

- string sessionKey

Return Value

- array:

    - struct - system

        - int "id"
        - string "name"
        - dateTime.iso8601 "last_checkin" - Last time server successfully checked in
        - dateTime.iso8601 "created" - Server registration time
        - dateTime.iso8601 "last_boot" - Last server boot time
        - int "extra_pkg_count" - Number of packages not belonging to any assigned channel
        - int "outdated_pkg_count" - Number of out-of-date packages

39.92 obtainReactivationKey

Description

Obtains a reactivation key for this server.

Parameters

- string sessionKey
- int serverId

Return Value

- string

39.93 obtainReactivationKey

Description

Obtains a reactivation key for this server.

Available since: 10.10

Parameters

- string systemid - systemid file

Return Value

- string

39.94 provisionSystem

Description

Provision a system using the specified kickstart profile.

Parameters

- string sessionKey
- int serverId - ID of the system to be provisioned.
- string profileName - Kickstart profile to use.

Return Value

- int - ID of the action scheduled, otherwise exception thrown on error

39.95 provisionSystem

Description

Provision a system using the specified kickstart profile.

Parameters

- string sessionKey
- int serverId - ID of the system to be provisioned.
- string profileName - Kickstart profile to use.
- dateTime.iso8601 earliestDate

Return Value

- int - ID of the action scheduled, otherwise exception thrown on error

39.96 provisionVirtualGuest

Description

Provision a guest on the host specified. Defaults to: memory = 512MB, vcpu = 1, storage = 3GB, mac_address = random.

Parameters

- string sessionKey
- int serverId - ID of host to provision guest on.
- string guestName
- string profileName - Kickstart profile to use.

Return Value

- int - 1 on success, exception thrown otherwise.

39.97 provisionVirtualGuest

Description

Provision a guest on the host specified. This schedules the guest for creation and will begin the provisioning process when the host checks in or if OSAD is enabled will begin immediately. Defaults to mac_address = random.

Parameters

- string sessionKey
- int serverId - ID of host to provision guest on.
- string guestName
- string profileName - Kickstart Profile to use.
- int memoryMb - Memory to allocate to the guest
- int vcpus - Number of virtual CPUs to allocate to the guest.
- int storageGb - Size of the guests disk image.

Return Value

- int - 1 on success, exception thrown otherwise.

39.98 provisionVirtualGuest

Description

Provision a guest on the host specified. This schedules the guest for creation and will begin the provisioning process when the host checks in or if OSAD is enabled will begin immediately.

Parameters

- string sessionKey
- int serverId - ID of host to provision guest on.
- string guestName
- string profileName - Kickstart Profile to use.
- int memoryMb - Memory to allocate to the guest
- int vcpus - Number of virtual CPUs to allocate to the guest.
- int storageGb - Size of the guests disk image.
- string macAddress - macAddress to give the guest's virtual networking hardware.

Return Value

- int - 1 on success, exception thrown otherwise.

39.99 removeEntitlements

Description

Remove addon entitlements from a server. Entitlements a server does not have are quietly ignored.

Parameters

- string sessionKey
- int serverId
- array:

  - string - entitlement_label

Return Value

- int - 1 on success, exception thrown otherwise.

39.100   scheduleApplyErrata

Description

Schedules an action to apply errata updates to multiple systems.
Available since: 13.0

Parameters

- string sessionKey
- array:

  - int - serverId
- array:

  - int - errataId

Return Value

- array:

  - int - actionId

39.101   scheduleApplyErrata

Description

Schedules an action to apply errata updates to multiple systems at a given date/time.

Available since: 13.0

Parameters

- string sessionKey
- array:

  - int - serverId
- array:

  - int - errataId
- dateTime.iso8601 earliestOccurrence

Return Value

- array:

  - int - actionId

39.102 scheduleApplyErrata

Description

Schedules an action to apply errata updates to a system.

Available since: 13.0

Parameters

- string sessionKey
- int serverId
- array:

    - int - errataId

Return Value

- array:

    - int - actionId

39.103 scheduleApplyErrata

Description

Schedules an action to apply errata updates to a system at a given date/time.
Available since: 13.0

Parameters

- string sessionKey
- int serverId
- array:

    - int - errataId
- dateTime.iso8601 earliestOccurrence

Return Value

- array:

    - int - actionId

39.104 scheduleCertificateUpdate

Description

Schedule update of client certificate

Parameters

- string sessionKey
- int serverId

Return Value

- int actionId - The action id of the scheduled action

39.105 scheduleCertificateUpdate

Description

Schedule update of client certificate at given date and time

Parameters

- string sessionKey
- int serverId
- dateTime.iso860 date

Return Value

- int actionId - The action id of the scheduled action

39.106 scheduleDistUpgrade

Description

Schedule a dist upgrade for a system. This call takes a list of channel labels that the system will be subscribed to before performing the dist upgrade. Note: You can seriously damage your system with this call, use it only if you really know what you are doing! Make sure that the list of channel labels is complete and in any case do a dry run before scheduling an actual dist upgrade.

Parameters

- string sessionKey
- int serverId

- array:

    - string - channels
- boolean dryRun
- dateTime.iso8601 earliest

Return Value

- int actionId - The action id of the scheduled action

39.107 scheduleGuestAction

Description

Schedules a guest action for the specified virtual guest for a given date/time.

Parameters

- string sessionKey
- int sid - the system Id of the guest
- string state - One of the following actions 'start', 'suspend', 'resume', 'restart', 'shut-down'.
- dateTime.iso8601 date - the time/date to schedule the action

Return Value

- int actionId - The action id of the scheduled action

39.108 scheduleGuestAction

Description

Schedules a guest action for the specified virtual guest for the current time.

Parameters

- string sessionKey
- int sid - the system Id of the guest
- string state - One of the following actions 'start', 'suspend', 'resume', 'restart', 'shut-down'.

Return Value

- int actionId - The action id of the scheduled action

39.109   scheduleHardwareRefresh

Description

Schedule a hardware refresh for a system.

Available since: 13.0

Parameters

- string sessionKey
- int serverId
- dateTime.iso8601 earliestOccurrence

Return Value

- int actionId - The action id of the scheduled action

39.110   schedulePackageInstall

Description

Schedule package installation for several systems.

Parameters

- string sessionKey
- array:

  - int - serverId
- array:

  - int - packageId
- dateTime.iso8601 earliestOccurrence

Return Value

- array:

    - int - actionId

39.111 schedulePackageInstall

Description

Schedule package installation for a system.
Available since: 13.0

Parameters

- string sessionKey
- int serverId
- array:

    - int - packageId
- dateTime.iso8601 earliestOccurrence

Return Value

- int actionId - The action id of the scheduled action

39.112 schedulePackageInstallByNevra

Description

Schedule package installation for several systems.

Parameters

- string sessionKey
- array:

    - int - serverId
- array:

    - struct - Package nevra

- string "package_name"
- string "package_epoch"
- string "package_version"
- string "package_release"
- string "package_arch"
- dateTime.iso8601 earliestOccurrence

Return Value

- array:

  - int - actionId

39.113 schedulePackageInstallByNevra

Description

Schedule package installation for a system.

Parameters

- string sessionKey
- int serverId
- array:

  - struct - Package nevra

    - string "package_name"
    - string "package_epoch"
    - string "package_version"
    - string "package_release"
    - string "package_arch"
- dateTime.iso8601 earliestOccurrence

Return Value

* int actionId - The action id of the scheduled action

39.114 schedulePackageRefresh

Description

Schedule a package list refresh for a system.

Parameters

* string sessionKey
* int serverId
* dateTime.iso8601 earliestOccurrence

Return Value

* int - ID of the action scheduled, otherwise exception thrown on error

39.115 schedulePackageRemove

Description

Schedule package removal for several systems.

Parameters

* string sessionKey
* array:

    * int - serverId
* array:

    * int - packageId
* dateTime.iso8601 earliestOccurrence

Return Value

- array:

    - int - actionId

39.116 schedulePackageRemove

Description

Schedule package removal for a system.

Parameters

- string sessionKey
- int serverId
- array:

    - int - packageId
- dateTime.iso8601 earliestOccurrence

Return Value

- int actionId - The action id of the scheduled action

39.117 schedulePackageRemoveByNevra

Description

Schedule package removal for several systems.

Parameters

- string sessionKey
- array:

    - int - serverId
- array:

    - struct - Package nevra

- string "package_name"
- string "package_epoch"
- string "package_version"
- string "package_release"
- string "package_arch"
- dateTime.iso8601 earliestOccurrence

Return Value

- array:

    - int - actionId

39.118 schedulePackageRemoveByNevra

Description

Schedule package removal for a system.

Parameters

- string sessionKey
- int serverId
- array:

    - struct - Package nevra

        - string "package_name"
        - string "package_epoch"
        - string "package_version"
        - string "package_release"
        - string "package_arch"
- dateTime.iso8601 earliestOccurrence

Return Value

- array:

    - int - actionId

39.119 scheduleReboot

Description

Schedule a reboot for a system.

Available since: 13.0

Parameters

- string sessionKey
- int serverId
- dateTime.iso860 earliestOccurrence

Return Value

- int actionId - The action id of the scheduled action

39.120 scheduleSPMigration

Description

Schedule a Service Pack migration for a system. This call is the recommended and supported way of migrating a system to the next Service Pack. It will automatically find all mandatory product channels below a given target base channel and subscribe the system accordingly. Any additional optional channels can be subscribed by providing their labels.

Parameters

- string sessionKey
- int serverId
- string baseChannelLabel

- array:

    - string - optionalChildChannels
- boolean dryRun
- dateTime.iso8601 earliest

Return Value

- int actionId - The action id of the scheduled action

39.121 scheduleSPMigration

Description

Schedule a Service Pack migration for a system. This call is the recommended and supported way of migrating a system to the next Service Pack. It will automatically find all mandatory product channels below a given target base channel and subscribe the system accordingly. Any additional optional channels can be subscribed by providing their labels.

Parameters

- string sessionKey
- int serverId
- string targetIdent
- string baseChannelLabel
- array:

    - string - optionalChildChannels
- boolean dryRun
- dateTime.iso8601 earliest

Return Value

- int actionId - The action id of the scheduled action

39.122 scheduleScriptRun

Description

Schedule a script to run.

Parameters

- string sessionKey
- string label
- array:

  - int - System IDs of the servers to run the script on.
- string username - User to run script as.
- string groupname - Group to run script as.
- int timeout - Seconds to allow the script to run before timing out.
- string script - Contents of the script to run.
- dateTime.iso8601 earliestOccurrence - Earliest the script can run.

Return Value

- int - ID of the script run action created. Can be used to fetch results with system.getScriptResults.

39.123 scheduleScriptRun

Description

Schedule a script to run.

Parameters

- string sessionKey
- array:

  - int - System IDs of the servers to run the script on.
- string username - User to run script as.
- string groupname - Group to run script as.
- int timeout - Seconds to allow the script to run before timing out.
- string script - Contents of the script to run.
- dateTime.iso8601 earliestOccurrence - Earliest the script can run.

Return Value

- int - ID of the script run action created. Can be used to fetch results with system.getScriptResults.

39.124 scheduleScriptRun

Description

Schedule a script to run.

Parameters

- string sessionKey
- int serverId - ID of the server to run the script on.
- string username - User to run script as.
- string groupname - Group to run script as.
- int timeout - Seconds to allow the script to run before timing out.
- string script - Contents of the script to run.
- dateTime.iso8601 earliestOccurrence - Earliest the script can run.

Return Value

- int - ID of the script run action created. Can be used to fetch results with system.getScriptResults.

39.125 scheduleScriptRun

Description

Schedule a script to run.

Parameters

- string sessionKey
- string label
- int serverId - ID of the server to run the script on.
- string username - User to run script as.
- string groupname - Group to run script as.
- int timeout - Seconds to allow the script to run before timing out.

- string script - Contents of the script to run.
- dateTime.iso8601 earliestOccurrence - Earliest the script can run.

Return Value

- int - ID of the script run action created. Can be used to fetch results with system.getScriptResults.

39.126 scheduleSyncPackagesWithSystem

Description

Sync packages from a source system to a target.
Available since: 13.0

Parameters

- string sessionKey
- int targetServerId - Target system to apply package changes to.
- int sourceServerId - Source system to retrieve package state from.
- array:

    - int - packageId - Package IDs to be synced.
- dateTime.iso8601 date - Date to schedule action for

Return Value

- int actionId - The action id of the scheduled action

39.127 searchByName

Description

Returns a list of system IDs whose name matches the supplied regular expression(defined by Java representation of regular expressions)

Parameters

- string sessionKey
- string regexp - A regular expression

Return Value

- array:

    - struct - system

        - int "id"
        - string "name"
        - dateTime.iso8601 "last_checkin" - Last time server successfully checked in
        - dateTime.iso8601 "created" - Server registration time
        - dateTime.iso8601 "last_boot" - Last server boot time
        - int "extra_pkg_count" - Number of packages not belonging to any assigned channel
        - int "outdated_pkg_count" - Number of out-of-date packages

39.128 sendOsaPing

Description

send a ping to a system using OSA

Parameters

- string sessionKey
- int serverId

Return Value

- int - 1 on success, exception thrown otherwise.

39.129 setBaseChannel

Description

Assigns the server to a new baseChannel.

Deprecated - being replaced by system.setBaseChannel(string sessionKey, int serverId, string channelLabel)

Parameters

- string sessionKey
- int serverId
- int channelId

Return Value

- int - 1 on success, exception thrown otherwise.

39.130 setBaseChannel

Description

Assigns the server to a new base channel. If the user provides an empty string for the channelLabel, the current base channel and all child channels will be removed from the system. Changes to channel assignments on salt managed systems will take effect at next highstate application.

Parameters

- string sessionKey
- int serverId
- string channelLabel

Return Value

- int - 1 on success, exception thrown otherwise.

39.131 setChildChannels

Description

Subscribe the given server to the child channels provided. This method will unsubscribe the server from any child channels that the server is currently subscribed to, but that are not included in the list. The user may provide either a list of channel ids (int) or a list of channel labels (string) as input. Changes to channel assignments on salt managed systems will take effect at next highstate application.

Parameters

- string sessionKey
- int serverId
- array:

    - int (deprecated) or string - channelId (deprecated) or channelLabel

Return Value

- int - 1 on success, exception thrown otherwise.

39.132 setCustomValues

Description

Set custom values for the specified server.

Parameters

- string sessionKey
- int serverId
- struct - Map of custom labels to custom values

    - string "custom info label"
    - string "value"

Return Value

- int - 1 on success, exception thrown otherwise.

39.133 setDetails

Description

Set server details. All arguments are optional and will only be modified if included in the struct.

Parameters

- string sessionKey
- int serverId - ID of server to lookup details for.
- struct - server details

  - string "profile_name" - System's profile name
  - string "base_entitlement" - System's base entitlement label. (enterprise_entitled or unentitle)
  - boolean "auto_errata_update" - True if system has auto errata updates enabled
  - string "description" - System description
  - string "address1" - System's address line 1.
  - string "address2" - System's address line 2.
  - string "city"
  - string "state"
  - string "country"
  - string "building"
  - string "room"
  - string "rack"
  - string "contact_method" - One of the following:
    - default
    - ssh-push
    - ssh-push-tunnel

Return Value

- int - 1 on success, exception thrown otherwise.

39.134 setGroupMembership

Description

Set a servers membership in a given group.

Parameters

- string sessionKey
- int serverId

- int serverGroupId
- boolean member - '1' to assign the given server to the given server group, '0' to remove the given server from the given server group.

Return Value

- int - 1 on success, exception thrown otherwise.

39.135 setGuestCpus

Description

Schedule an action of a guest's host, to set that guest's CPU allocation

Parameters

- string sessionKey
- int sid - The guest's system id
- int numOfCpus - The number of virtual cpus to allocate to the guest

Return Value

- int actionID - the action Id for the schedule action on the host system.

39.136 setGuestMemory

Description

Schedule an action of a guest's host, to set that guest's memory allocation

Parameters

- string sessionKey
- int sid - The guest's system id
- int memory - The amount of memory to allocate to the guest

Return Value

- int actionID - the action Id for the schedule action on the host system.

39.137 setLockStatus

Description

Set server lock status.

Parameters

- string sessionKey
- int serverId
- boolean lockStatus - true to lock the system, false to unlock the system.

Return Value

- int - 1 on success, exception thrown otherwise.

39.138 setPrimaryInterface

Description

Sets new primary network interface

Parameters

- string sessionKey
- int serverId
- string interfaceName

Return Value

- int - 1 on success, exception thrown otherwise.

39.139 setProfileName

Description

Set the profile name for the server.

Parameters

- string sessionKey
- int serverId
- string name - Name of the profile.

Return Value

- int - 1 on success, exception thrown otherwise.

39.140 setVariables

Description

Sets a list of kickstart variables in the cobbler system record for the specified server. Note: This call assumes that a system record exists in cobbler for the given system and will raise an XMLRPC fault if that is not the case. To create a system record over xmlrpc use system.createSystemRecord To create a system record in the Web UI please go to System -> <Specified System> -> Provisioning -> Select a Kickstart profile -> Create Cobbler System Record.

Parameters

- string sessionKey
- int serverId
- boolean netboot
- array:

  - struct - kickstart variable

- string "key"
- string or int "value"

Return Value

- int - 1 on success, exception thrown otherwise.

39.141 tagLatestSnapshot

Description

Tags latest system snapshot

Parameters

- string sessionKey
- int serverId
- string tagName

Return Value

- int - 1 on success, exception thrown otherwise.

39.142 unentitle

Description

Unentitle the system completely

Parameters

- string systemid - systemid file

Return Value

- int - 1 on success, exception thrown otherwise.

39.143 upgradeEntitlement

Description

Adds an entitlement to a given server.

Parameters

- string sessionKey
- int serverId
- string entitlementName - One of: 'enterprise_entitled' or 'virtualization_host'.

Return Value

- int - 1 on success, exception thrown otherwise.

39.144 whoRegistered

Description

Returns information about the user who registered the system

Parameters

- string sessionKey
- int sid - Id of the system in question

Return Value

- struct - user

  - int "id"
  - string "login"

- string "login_uc" - upper case version of the login
- boolean "enabled" - true if user is enabled, false if the user is disabled

40 system.config

Provides methods to access and modify many aspects of configuration channels and server association. basically system.config name space

40.1 addChannels

Description

> Given a list of servers and configuration channels, this method appends the configuration channels to either the top or the bottom (whichever you specify) of a system's subscribed configuration channels list. The ordering of the configuration channels provided in the add list is maintained while adding. If one of the configuration channels in the 'add' list has been previously subscribed by a server, the subscribed channel will be re-ranked to the appropriate place.

Parameters

- string sessionKey
- array:

    - int - IDs of the systems to add the channels to.
- array:

    - string - List of configuration channel labels in the ranked order.
- boolean addToTop

    - true - to prepend the given channels list to the top of the configuration channels list of a server
    - false - to append the given channels list to the bottom of the configuration channels list of a server

Return Value

- int - 1 on success, exception thrown otherwise.

40.2 createOrUpdatePath

Description

Create a new file (text or binary) or directory with the given path, or update an existing path on a server.

Available since: 10.2

Parameters

- string sessionKey
- int serverId
- string path - the configuration file/directory path
- boolean isDir
    - True - if the path is a directory
    - False - if the path is a file
- struct - path info

    - string "contents" - Contents of the file (text or base64 encoded if binary) ((only for non-directories)
    - boolean "contents_enc64" - Identifies base64 encoded content (default: disabled, only for non-directories).
    - string "owner" - Owner of the file/directory.
    - string "group" - Group name of the file/directory.
    - string "permissions" - Octal file/directory permissions (eg: 644)
    - string "macro-start-delimiter" - Config file macro end delimiter. Use null or empty string to accept the default. (only for non-directories)
    - string "macro-end-delimiter" - Config file macro end delimiter. Use null or empty string to accept the default. (only for non-directories)
    - string "selinux_ctx" - SeLinux context (optional)
    - int "revision" - next revision number, auto increment for null
    - boolean "binary" - mark the binary content, if True, base64 encoded content is expected (only for non-directories)

- int commitToLocal

  - 1 - to commit configuration files to the system's local override configuration channel

    - 0 - to commit configuration files to the system's sandbox configuration channel

Return Value

- struct - Configuration Revision information

  - string "type"

    - file

      - directory

      - symlink

  - string "path" - File Path

  - string "target_path" - Symbolic link Target File Path. Present for Symbolic links only.

  - string "channel" - Channel Name

  - string "contents" - File contents (base64 encoded according to the contents_enc64 attribute)

  - boolean "contents_enc64" - Identifies base64 encoded content

  - int "revision" - File Revision

  - dateTime.iso8601 "creation" - Creation Date

  - dateTime.iso8601 "modified" - Last Modified Date

  - string "owner" - File Owner. Present for files or directories only.

  - string "group" - File Group. Present for files or directories only.

  - int "permissions" - File Permissions (Deprecated). Present for files or directories only.

  - string "permissions_mode" - File Permissions. Present for files or directories only.

  - string "selinux_ctx" - SELinux Context (optional).

  - boolean "binary" - true/false , Present for files only.

  - string "sha256" - File's sha256 signature. Present for files only.

- string "macro-start-delimiter" - Macro start delimiter for a config file. Present for text files only.
- string "macro-end-delimiter" - Macro end delimiter for a config file. Present for text files only.

40.3   createOrUpdateSymlink

Description

Create a new symbolic link with the given path, or update an existing path.

Available since: 10.2

Parameters

- string sessionKey
- int serverId
- string path - the configuration file/directory path
- struct - path info

    - string "target_path" - The target path for the symbolic link
    - string "selinux_ctx" - SELinux Security context (optional)
    - int "revision" - next revision number, auto increment for null
- int commitToLocal
  - 1 - to commit configuration files to the system's local override configuration channel
    - 0 - to commit configuration files to the system's sandbox configuration channel

Return Value

- struct - Configuration Revision information

    - string "type"
      - file
        - directory
        - symlink
    - string "path" - File Path
    - string "target_path" - Symbolic link Target File Path. Present for Symbolic links only.
    - string "channel" - Channel Name

- string "contents" - File contents (base64 encoded according to the contents_enc64 attribute)
- boolean "contents_enc64" - Identifies base64 encoded content
- int "revision" - File Revision
- dateTime.iso8601 "creation" - Creation Date
- dateTime.iso8601 "modified" - Last Modified Date
- string "owner" - File Owner. Present for files or directories only.
- string "group" - File Group. Present for files or directories only.
- int "permissions" - File Permissions (Deprecated). Present for files or directories only.
- string "permissions_mode" - File Permissions. Present for files or directories only.
- string "selinux_ctx" - SELinux Context (optional).
- boolean "binary" - true/false , Present for files only.
- string "sha256" - File's sha256 signature. Present for files only.
- string "macro-start-delimiter" - Macro start delimiter for a config file. Present for text files only.
- string "macro-end-delimiter" - Macro end delimiter for a config file. Present for text files only.

40.4 deleteFiles

Description

Removes file paths from a local or sandbox channel of a server.

Parameters

- string sessionKey
- int serverId
- array:

  - string - paths to remove.
- boolean deleteFromLocal
  - True - to delete configuration file paths from the system's local override configuration channel
    - False - to delete configuration file paths from the system's sandbox configuration channel

Return Value

- int - 1 on success, exception thrown otherwise.

40.5 deployAll

Description

Schedules a deploy action for all the configuration files on the given list of systems.

Parameters

- string sessionKey
- array:

  - int - id of the systems to schedule configuration files deployment
- dateTime.iso8601 date - Earliest date for the deploy action.

Return Value

- int - 1 on success, exception thrown otherwise.

40.6 listChannels

Description

List all global configuration channels associated to a system in the order of their ranking.

Parameters

- string sessionKey
- int serverId

Return Value

- array:

  - struct - Configuration Channel information

    - int "id"
    - int "orgId"
    - string "label"

- string "name"
- string "description"
- struct "configChannelType"
- struct - Configuration Channel Type information

    - int "id"
    - string "label"
    - string "name"
    - int "priority"

40.7 listFiles

Description

Return the list of files in a given channel.

Parameters

- string sessionKey
- int serverId
- int listLocal
    - 1 - to return configuration files in the system's local override configuration channel
    - 0 - to return configuration files in the system's sandbox configuration channel

Return Value

- array:

    - struct - Configuration File information

        - string "type"
            - file
            - directory
            - symlink
        - string "path" - File Path
        - string "channel_label" - the label of the central configuration channel that has this file. Note this entry only shows up if the file has not been overridden by a central channel.

- struct "channel_type"
  - struct - Configuration Channel Type information

    - int "id"
    - string "label"
    - string "name"
    - int "priority"
  - dateTime.iso8601 "last_modified" - Last Modified Date

40.8 lookupFileInfo

Description

Given a list of paths and a server, returns details about the latest revisions of the paths.
Available since: 10.2

Parameters

- string sessionKey
- int serverId
- array:

  - string - paths to lookup on.
- int searchLocal
  - 1 - to search configuration file paths in the system's local override configuration
    or systems subscribed central channels
  - 0 - to search configuration file paths in the system's sandbox configuration chan-
    nel

Return Value

- array:

  - struct - Configuration Revision information

    - string "type"
      - file
      - directory
      - symlink

- string "path" - File Path
- string "target_path" - Symbolic link Target File Path. Present for Symbolic links only.
- string "channel" - Channel Name
- string "contents" - File contents (base64 encoded according to the contents_enc64 attribute)
- boolean "contents_enc64" - Identifies base64 encoded content
- int "revision" - File Revision
- dateTime.iso8601 "creation" - Creation Date
- dateTime.iso8601 "modified" - Last Modified Date
- string "owner" - File Owner. Present for files or directories only.
- string "group" - File Group. Present for files or directories only.
- int "permissions" - File Permissions (Deprecated). Present for files or directories only.
- string "permissions_mode" - File Permissions. Present for files or directories only.
- string "selinux_ctx" - SELinux Context (optional).
- boolean "binary" - true/false , Present for files only.
- string "sha256" - File's sha256 signature. Present for files only.
- string "macro-start-delimiter" - Macro start delimiter for a config file. Present for text files only.
- string "macro-end-delimiter" - Macro end delimiter for a config file. Present for text files only.

40.9 removeChannels

Description

Remove config channels from the given servers.

Parameters

- string sessionKey
- array:

    - int - the IDs of the systems from which you would like to remove configuration channels..

- array:

    - string - List of configuration channel labels to remove.

Return Value

- int - 1 on success, exception thrown otherwise.

40.10 setChannels

Description

Replace the existing set of config channels on the given servers. Channels are ranked according to their order in the configChannelLabels array.

Parameters

- string sessionKey
- array:

    - int - IDs of the systems to set the channels on.

- array:

    - string - List of configuration channel labels in the ranked order.

Return Value

- int - 1 on success, exception thrown otherwise.

41 system.crash

Provides methods to access and modify software crash information.

41.1 createCrashNote

Description

Create a crash note

Parameters

- string sessionKey
- int crashId
- string subject
- string details

Return Value

- int - 1 on success, exception thrown otherwise.

41.2 deleteCrash

Description

Delete a crash with given crash id.

Parameters

- string sessionKey
- int crashId

Return Value

- int - 1 on success, exception thrown otherwise.

41.3 deleteCrashNote

Description

Delete a crash note

Parameters

- string sessionKey
- int crashNoteId

Return Value

- int - 1 on success, exception thrown otherwise.

41.4 getCrashCountInfo

Description

Return date of last software crashes report for given system

Parameters

- string sessionKey
- int serverId

Return Value

- struct - Crash Count Information

  - int "total_count" - Total number of software crashes for a system
  - int "unique_count" - Number of unique software crashes for a system
  - dateTime.iso8601 "last_report" - Date of the last software crash report

41.5 getCrashFile

Description

Download a crash file.

Parameters

- string sessionKey
- int crashFileId

Return Value

- base64 - base64 encoded crash file.

41.6 getCrashFileUrl

Description

Get a crash file download url.

Parameters

- string sessionKey
- int crashFileId

Return Value

- string - The crash file download url

41.7 getCrashNotesForCrash

Description

List crash notes for crash

Parameters

- string sessionKey
- int crashId

Return Value

- array:
    - struct - crashNote
        - int "id"
        - string "subject"

- string "details"
- string "updated"

41.8 getCrashOverview

Description

Get Software Crash Overview

Parameters

- string sessionKey

Return Value

- array:

    - struct - crash

        - string "uuid" - Crash UUID
        - string "component" - Package component (set if unique and non empty)
        - int "crash_count" - Number of crashes occurred
        - int "system_count" - Number of systems affected
        - dateTime.iso8601 "last_report" - Last crash occurence

41.9 getCrashesByUuid

Description

List software crashes with given UUID

Parameters

- string sessionKey
- string uuid

Return Value

- array:

    - struct - crash

- int "server_id" - ID of the server the crash occurred on
- string "server_name" - Name of the server the crash occurred on
- int "crash_id" - ID of the crash with given UUID
- int "crash_count" - Number of times the crash with given UUID occurred
- string "crash_component" - Crash component
- dateTime.iso8601 "last_report" - Last crash occurence

41.10 listSystemCrashFiles

Description

Return list of crash files for given crash id.

Parameters

- string sessionKey
- int crashId

Return Value

- array:

    - struct - crashFile

        - int "id"
        - string "filename"
        - string "path"
        - int "filesize"
        - boolean "is_uploaded"
        - date "created"
        - date "modified"

41.11 listSystemCrashes

Description

Return list of software crashes for a system.

Parameters

- string sessionKey
- int serverId

Return Value

- array:

    - struct - crash

        - int "id"
        - string "crash"
        - string "path"
        - int "count"
        - string "uuid"
        - string "analyzer"
        - string "architecture"
        - string "cmdline"
        - string "component"
        - string "executable"
        - string "kernel"
        - string "reason"
        - string "username"
        - date "created"
        - date "modified"

42 system.custominfo

Provides methods to access and modify custom system information.

42.1 createKey

Description

Create a new custom key

Parameters

- string sessionKey
- string keyLabel - new key's label
- string keyDescription - new key's description

Return Value

- int - 1 on success, exception thrown otherwise.

42.2 deleteKey

Description

Delete an existing custom key and all systems' values for the key.

Parameters

- string sessionKey
- string keyLabel - new key's label

Return Value

- int - 1 on success, exception thrown otherwise.

42.3 listAllKeys

Description

List the custom information keys defined for the user's organization.

Parameters

- string sessionKey

Return Value

- array:

  - struct - custom info

    - int "id"
    - string "label"
    - string "description"
    - int "system_count"
    - dateTime.iso8601 "last_modified"

42.4 updateKey

Description

Update description of a custom key

Parameters

- string sessionKey
- string keyLabel - key to change
- string keyDescription - new key's description

Return Value

- int - 1 on success, exception thrown otherwise.

43 system.provisioning.snapshot

Provides methods to access and delete system snapshots.

43.1 addTagToSnapshot

Description

> Adds tag to snapshot

Parameters

- string sessionKey
- int snapshotId - Id of the snapshot
- string tag - Name of the snapshot tag

Return Value

- int - 1 on success, exception thrown otherwise.

43.2 deleteSnapshot

Description

> Deletes a snapshot with the given snapshot id
> Available since: 10.1

Parameters

- string sessionKey
- int snapshotId - Id of snapshot to delete

Return Value

- int - 1 on success, exception thrown otherwise.

43.3 deleteSnapshots

Description

> Deletes all snapshots across multiple systems based on the given date criteria. For example,

- If the user provides startDate only, all snapshots created either on or after the date provided will be removed.

- If user provides startDate and endDate, all snapshots created on or between the dates provided will be removed.

- If the user doesn't provide a startDate and endDate, all snapshots will be removed.

Available since: 10.1

Parameters

- string sessionKey
- struct - date details

    - dateTime.iso8601 "startDate" - Optional, unless endDate is provided.
    - dateTime.iso8601 "endDate" - Optional.

Return Value

- int - 1 on success, exception thrown otherwise.

43.4 deleteSnapshots

Description

Deletes all snapshots for a given system based on the date criteria. For example,

- If the user provides startDate only, all snapshots created either on or after the date provided will be removed.

- If user provides startDate and endDate, all snapshots created on or between the dates provided will be removed.

- If the user doesn't provide a startDate and endDate, all snapshots associated with the server will be removed.

Available since: 10.1

Parameters

- string sessionKey
- int sid - system id of system to delete snapshots for
- struct - date details

- dateTime.iso8601 "startDate" - Optional, unless endDate is provided.
- dateTime.iso8601 "endDate" - Optional.

Return Value

- int - 1 on success, exception thrown otherwise.

43.5 listSnapshotConfigFiles

Description

List the config files associated with a snapshot.
Available since: 10.2

Parameters

- string sessionKey
- int snapId

Return Value

- array:

    - struct - Configuration Revision information

        - string "type"
            - file
            - directory
            - symlink
        - string "path" - File Path
        - string "target_path" - Symbolic link Target File Path. Present for Symbolic links only.
        - string "channel" - Channel Name
        - string "contents" - File contents (base64 encoded according to the contents_enc64 attribute)
        - boolean "contents_enc64" - Identifies base64 encoded content
        - int "revision" - File Revision
        - dateTime.iso8601 "creation" - Creation Date

- dateTime.iso8601 "modified" - Last Modified Date

- string "owner" - File Owner. Present for files or directories only.

- string "group" - File Group. Present for files or directories only.

- int "permissions" - File Permissions (Deprecated). Present for files or directories only.

- string "permissions_mode" - File Permissions. Present for files or directories only.

- string "selinux_ctx" - SELinux Context (optional).

- boolean "binary" - true/false , Present for files only.

- string "sha256" - File's sha256 signature. Present for files only.

- string "macro-start-delimiter" - Macro start delimiter for a config file. Present for text files only.

- string "macro-end-delimiter" - Macro end delimiter for a config file. Present for text files only.

43.6 listSnapshotPackages

Description

List the packages associated with a snapshot.

Available since: 10.1

Parameters

- string sessionKey
- int snapId

Return Value

- array:

  - struct - package nvera

    - string "name"
    - string "epoch"
    - string "version"

- string "release"
- string "arch"

43.7 listSnapshots

Description

List snapshots for a given system. A user may optionally provide a start and end date to narrow the snapshots that will be listed. For example,

- If the user provides startDate only, all snapshots created either on or after the date provided will be returned.

- If user provides startDate and endDate, all snapshots created on or between the dates provided will be returned.

- If the user doesn't provide a startDate and endDate, all snapshots associated with the server will be returned.

Available since: 10.1

Parameters

- string sessionKey
- int serverId
- struct - date details

    - dateTime.iso8601 "startDate" - Optional, unless endDate is provided.
    - dateTime.iso8601 "endDate" - Optional.

Return Value

- array:

    - struct - server snapshot

        - int "id"
        - string "reason" - the reason for the snapshot's existence
        - dateTime.iso8601 "created"
        - array "channels"

- string - labels of channels associated with the snapshot
  - array "groups"
    - string - Names of server groups associated with the snapshot
  - array "entitlements"
    - string - Names of system entitlements associated with the snapshot
  - array "config_channels"
    - string - Labels of config channels the snapshot is associated with.
  - array "tags"
    - string - Tag names associated with this snapshot.
  - string "Invalid_reason" - If the snapshot is invalid, this is the reason (optional).

43.8 rollbackToSnapshot

Description

Rollbacks server to snapshot

Parameters

- string sessionKey
- int serverId
- int snapshotId - Id of the snapshot

Return Value

- int - 1 on success, exception thrown otherwise.

43.9 rollbackToTag

Description

Rollbacks server to snapshot

Parameters

- string sessionKey
- int serverId
- string tagName - Name of the snapshot tag

Return Value

- int - 1 on success, exception thrown otherwise.

43.10   rollbackToTag

Description

Rollbacks server to snapshot

Parameters

- string sessionKey
- string tagName - Name of the snapshot tag

Return Value

- int - 1 on success, exception thrown otherwise.

44 system.scap

Provides methods to schedule SCAP scans and access the results.

44.1 deleteXccdfScan

Description

Delete OpenSCAP XCCDF Scan from Spacewalk database. Note that only those SCAP Scans can be deleted which have passed their retention period.

Parameters

- string sessionKey
- int Id of XCCDF scan (xid).

Return Value

- boolean - indicates success of the operation.

44.2 getXccdfScanDetails

Description

Get details of given OpenSCAP XCCDF scan.

Parameters

- string sessionKey
- int Id of XCCDF scan (xid).

Return Value

- struct - OpenSCAP XCCDF Scan

  - int "xid" - XCCDF TestResult id
  - int "sid" - serverId
  - int "action_id" - Id of the parent action.

- string "path" - Path to XCCDF document
- string "oscap_parameters" - oscap command-line arguments.
- string "test_result" - Identifier of XCCDF TestResult.
- string "benchmark" - Identifier of XCCDF Benchmark.
- string "benchmark_version" - Version of the Benchmark.
- string "profile" - Identifier of XCCDF Profile.
- string "profile_title" - Title of XCCDF Profile.
- dateTime.iso8601 "start_time" - Client machine time of scan start.
- dateTime.iso8601 "end_time" - Client machine time of scan completion.
- string "errors" - Stderr output of scan.
- bool "deletable" - Indicates whether the scan can be deleted.

44.3 getXccdfScanRuleResults

Description

Return a full list of RuleResults for given OpenSCAP XCCDF scan.

Parameters

- string sessionKey
- int Id of XCCDF scan (xid).

Return Value

- array:

    - struct - OpenSCAP XCCDF RuleResult

        - string "idref" - idref from XCCDF document.
        - string "result" - Result of evaluation.
        - string "idents" - Comma separated list of XCCDF idents.

44.4 listXccdfScans

Description

Return a list of finished OpenSCAP scans for a given system.

Parameters

- string sessionKey
- int serverId

Return Value

- array:

    - struct - OpenSCAP XCCDF Scan

        - int "xid" - XCCDF TestResult ID
        - string "profile" - XCCDF Profile
        - string "path" - Path to XCCDF document
        - dateTime.iso8601 "completed" - Scan completion time

44.5 scheduleXccdfScan

Description

Schedule OpenSCAP scan.

Parameters

- string sessionKey
- array:

    - int - serverId
- string Path to xccdf content on targeted systems.
- string Additional parameters for oscap tool.

Return Value

- int - ID if SCAP action created.

44.6 scheduleXccdfScan

Description

Schedule OpenSCAP scan.

Parameters

- string sessionKey
- array:

  - int - serverId
- string Path to xccdf content on targeted systems.
- string Additional parameters for oscap tool.
- dateTime.iso8601 date - The date to schedule the action

Return Value

- int - ID if SCAP action created.

44.7 scheduleXccdfScan

Description

Schedule Scap XCCDF scan.

Parameters

- string sessionKey
- int serverId
- string Path to xccdf content on targeted system.
- string Additional parameters for oscap tool.

Return Value

- int - ID of the scap action created.

44.8 scheduleXccdfScan

Description

Schedule Scap XCCDF scan.

Parameters

- string sessionKey
- int serverId

- string Path to xccdf content on targeted system.
- string Additional parameters for oscap tool.
- dateTime.iso8601 date - The date to schedule the action

Return Value

- int - ID of the scap action created.

45 system.search

Provides methods to perform system search requests using the search server.

45.1 deviceDescription

Description

List the systems which match the device description.

Parameters

- string sessionKey
- string searchTerm

Return Value

- array:

    - struct - system

        - int "id"
        - string "name"
        - dateTime.iso8601 "last_checkin" - Last time server successfully checked in
        - string "hostname"
        - string "ip"
        - string "hw_description" - hw description if not null
        - string "hw_device_id" - hw device id if not null
        - string "hw_vendor_id" - hw vendor id if not null
        - string "hw_driver" - hw driver if not null

45.2 deviceDriver

Description

List the systems which match this device driver.

Parameters

- string sessionKey
- string searchTerm

Return Value

- array:

    - struct - system

        - int "id"
        - string "name"
        - dateTime.iso8601 "last_checkin" - Last time server successfully checked in
        - string "hostname"
        - string "ip"
        - string "hw_description" - hw description if not null
        - string "hw_device_id" - hw device id if not null
        - string "hw_vendor_id" - hw vendor id if not null
        - string "hw_driver" - hw driver if not null

45.3 deviceId

Description

List the systems which match this device id

Parameters

- string sessionKey
- string searchTerm

Return Value

- array:

    - struct - system

        - int "id"
        - string "name"
        - dateTime.iso8601 "last_checkin" - Last time server successfully checked in

- string "hostname"
- string "ip"
- string "hw_description" - hw description if not null
- string "hw_device_id" - hw device id if not null
- string "hw_vendor_id" - hw vendor id if not null
- string "hw_driver" - hw driver if not null

45.4 deviceVendorId

Description

List the systems which match this device vendor_id

Parameters

- string sessionKey
- string searchTerm

Return Value

- array:

    - struct - system

        - int "id"
        - string "name"
        - dateTime.iso8601 "last_checkin" - Last time server successfully checked in
        - string "hostname"
        - string "ip"
        - string "hw_description" - hw description if not null
        - string "hw_device_id" - hw device id if not null
        - string "hw_vendor_id" - hw vendor id if not null
        - string "hw_driver" - hw driver if not null

45.5 hostname

Description

List the systems which match this hostname

Parameters

- string sessionKey
- string searchTerm

Return Value

- array:

  - struct - system

    - int "id"
    - string "name"
    - dateTime.iso8601 "last_checkin" - Last time server successfully checked in
    - string "hostname"
    - string "ip"
    - string "hw_description" - hw description if not null
    - string "hw_device_id" - hw device id if not null
    - string "hw_vendor_id" - hw vendor id if not null
    - string "hw_driver" - hw driver if not null

45.6 ip

Description

List the systems which match this ip.

Parameters

- string sessionKey
- string searchTerm

Return Value

- array:

  - struct - system

    - int "id"
    - string "name"
    - dateTime.iso8601 "last_checkin" - Last time server successfully checked in

- string "hostname"
- string "ip"
- string "hw_description" - hw description if not null
- string "hw_device_id" - hw device id if not null
- string "hw_vendor_id" - hw vendor id if not null
- string "hw_driver" - hw driver if not null

45.7 nameAndDescription

Description

List the systems which match this name or description

Parameters

- string sessionKey
- string searchTerm

Return Value

- array:

    - struct - system

        - int "id"
        - string "name"
        - dateTime.iso8601 "last_checkin" - Last time server successfully checked in
        - string "hostname"
        - string "ip"
        - string "hw_description" - hw description if not null
        - string "hw_device_id" - hw device id if not null
        - string "hw_vendor_id" - hw vendor id if not null
        - string "hw_driver" - hw driver if not null

45.8 uuid

Description

List the systems which match this UUID

Parameters

- string sessionKey
- string searchTerm

Return Value

- array:

    - struct - system

        - int "id"
        - string "name"
        - dateTime.iso8601 "last_checkin" - Last time server successfully checked in
        - string "hostname"
        - string "ip"
        - string "hw_description" - hw description if not null
        - string "hw_device_id" - hw device id if not null
        - string "hw_vendor_id" - hw vendor id if not null
        - string "hw_driver" - hw driver if not null

46 systemgroup

Provides methods to access and modify system groups.

46.1 addOrRemoveAdmins

Description

Add or remove administrators to/from the given group. Satellite and Organization administrators are granted access to groups within their organization by default; therefore, users with those roles should not be included in the array provided. Caller must be an organization administrator.

Parameters

- string sessionKey
- string systemGroupName
- array:

    - string - loginName - User's loginName
- int add - 1 to add administrators, 0 to remove.

Return Value

- int - 1 on success, exception thrown otherwise.

46.2 addOrRemoveSystems

Description

Add/remove the given servers to a system group.

Parameters

- string sessionKey
- string systemGroupName
- array:

    - int - serverId
- boolean add - True to add to the group, False to remove.

Return Value

- int - 1 on success, exception thrown otherwise.

46.3 create

Description

Create a new system group.

Parameters

- string sessionKey
- string name - Name of the system group.
- string description - Description of the system group.

Return Value

- struct - Server Group

  - int "id"
  - string "name"
  - string "description"
  - int "org_id"
  - int "system_count"

46.4 delete

Description

Delete a system group.

Parameters

- string sessionKey
- string systemGroupName

Return Value

- int - 1 on success, exception thrown otherwise.

46.5 getDetails

Description

Retrieve details of a ServerGroup based on it's id

Parameters

- string sessionKey
- int systemGroupId

Return Value

- struct - Server Group

  - int "id"
  - string "name"
  - string "description"
  - int "org_id"
  - int "system_count"

46.6 getDetails

Description

Retrieve details of a ServerGroup based on it's name

Parameters

- string sessionKey
- string systemGroupName

Return Value

- struct - Server Group

  - int "id"
  - string "name"

- string "description"
- int "org_id"
- int "system_count"

46.7 listActiveSystemsInGroup

Description

Lists active systems within a server group

Parameters

- string sessionKey
- string systemGroupName

Return Value

- array:

    - int - server_id

46.8 listAdministrators

Description

Returns the list of users who can administer the given group. Caller must be a system group admin or an organization administrator.

Parameters

- string sessionKey
- string systemGroupName

Return Value

- array:

    - struct - user

        - int "id"
        - string "login"

- string "login_uc" - upper case version of the login
- boolean "enabled" - true if user is enabled, false if the user is disabled

46.9 listAllGroups

Description

Retrieve a list of system groups that are accessible by the logged in user.

Parameters

- string sessionKey

Return Value

- array:

    - struct - Server Group

        - int "id"
        - string "name"
        - string "description"
        - int "org_id"
        - int "system_count"

46.10 listGroupsWithNoAssociatedAdmins

Description

Returns a list of system groups that do not have an administrator. (who is not an organization administrator, as they have implicit access to system groups) Caller must be an organization administrator.

Parameters

- string sessionKey

Return Value

- array:

    - struct - Server Group

- int "id"
- string "name"
- string "description"
- int "org_id"
- int "system_count"

46.11 listInactiveSystemsInGroup

Description

Lists inactive systems within a server group using a specified inactivity time.

Parameters

- string sessionKey
- string systemGroupName
- int daysInactive - Number of days a system must not check in to be considered inactive.

Return Value

- array:

  - int - server_id

46.12 listInactiveSystemsInGroup

Description

Lists inactive systems within a server group using the default 1 day threshold.

Parameters

- string sessionKey
- string systemGroupName

Return Value

- array:

  - int - server_id

46.13 `listSystems`

Description

Return a list of systems associated with this system group. User must have access to this system group.

Parameters

- string sessionKey
- string systemGroupName

Return Value

- array:

  - struct - server details

    - int "id" - System id
    - string "profile_name"
    - string "base_entitlement" - System's base entitlement label
    - array "string"

      - addon_entitlements - System's addon entitlements labels, currently only 'virtualization_host'
    - boolean "auto_update" - True if system has auto errata updates enabled.
    - string "release" - The Operating System release (i.e. 4AS, 5Server
    - string "address1"
    - string "address2"
    - string "city"
    - string "state"
    - string "country"
    - string "building"

- string "room"
- string "rack"
- string "description"
- string "hostname"
- dateTime.iso8601 "last_boot"
- string "osa_status" - Either 'unknown', 'offline', or 'online'.
- boolean "lock_status" - True indicates that the system is locked. False indicates that the system is unlocked.
- string "virtualization" - Virtualization type - for virtual guests only (optional)
- string "contact_method" - One of the following:
    - default
    - ssh-push
    - ssh-push-tunnel

46.14 listSystemsMinimal

Description

Return a list of systems associated with this system group. User must have access to this system group.

Parameters

- string sessionKey
- string systemGroupName

Return Value

- array:

    - struct - system

        - int "id"
        - string "name"
        - dateTime.iso8601 "last_checkin" - Last time server successfully checked in
        - dateTime.iso8601 "created" - Server registration time
        - dateTime.iso8601 "last_boot" - Last server boot time

- int "extra_pkg_count" - Number of packages not belonging to any assigned channel
- int "outdated_pkg_count" - Number of out-of-date packages

46.15 scheduleApplyErrataToActive

Description

Schedules an action to apply errata updates to active systems from a group.

Available since: 13.0

Parameters

- string sessionKey
- string systemGroupName
- array:

    - int - errataId

Return Value

- array:

    - int - actionId

46.16 scheduleApplyErrataToActive

Description

Schedules an action to apply errata updates to active systems from a group at a given date/time.

Available since: 13.0

Parameters

- string sessionKey
- string systemGroupName
- array:

    - int - errataId
- dateTime.iso8601 earliestOccurrence

Return Value

- array:

    - int - actionId

46.17 update

Description

Update an existing system group.

Parameters

- string sessionKey
- string systemGroupName
- string description

Return Value

- struct - Server Group

    - int "id"
    - string "name"
    - string "description"
    - int "org_id"
    - int "system_count"

47 user

User namespace contains methods to access common user functions available from the web user interface.

47.1 addAssignedSystemGroup

Description

Add system group to user's list of assigned system groups.

Parameters

- string sessionKey
- string login - User's login name.
- string serverGroupName
- boolean setDefault - Should system group also be added to user's list of default system groups.

Return Value

- int - 1 on success, exception thrown otherwise.

47.2 addAssignedSystemGroups

Description

Add system groups to user's list of assigned system groups.

Parameters

- string sessionKey
- string login - User's login name.
- array:

  - string - serverGroupName
- boolean setDefault - Should system groups also be added to user's list of default system groups.

Return Value

- int - 1 on success, exception thrown otherwise.

47.3 addDefaultSystemGroup

Description

Add system group to user's list of default system groups.

Parameters

- string sessionKey
- string login - User's login name.
- string serverGroupName

Return Value

- int - 1 on success, exception thrown otherwise.

47.4 addDefaultSystemGroups

Description

Add system groups to user's list of default system groups.

Parameters

- string sessionKey
- string login - User's login name.
- array:

    - string - serverGroupName

Return Value

- int - 1 on success, exception thrown otherwise.

47.5 addRole

Description

Adds a role to a user.

Parameters

- string sessionKey
- string login - User login name to update.
- string role - Role label to add. Can be any of: satellite_admin, org_admin, channel_admin, config_admin, system_group_admin, or activation_key_admin.

Return Value

- int - 1 on success, exception thrown otherwise.

47.6 create

Description

Create a new user.

Parameters

- string sessionKey
- string desiredLogin - Desired login name, will fail if already in use.

- string desiredPassword
- string firstName
- string lastName
- string email - User's e-mail address.

Return Value

- int - 1 on success, exception thrown otherwise.

47.7 create

Description

Create a new user.

Parameters

- string sessionKey
- string desiredLogin - Desired login name, will fail if already in use.
- string desiredPassword
- string firstName
- string lastName
- string email - User's e-mail address.
- int usePamAuth - 1 if you wish to use PAM authentication for this user, 0 otherwise.

Return Value

- int - 1 on success, exception thrown otherwise.

47.8 delete

Description

Delete a user.

Parameters

- string sessionKey
- string login - User login name to delete.

Return Value

- int - 1 on success, exception thrown otherwise.

47.9 disable

Description

Disable a user.

Parameters

- string sessionKey
- string login - User login name to disable.

Return Value

- int - 1 on success, exception thrown otherwise.

47.10 enable

Description

Enable a user.

Parameters

- string sessionKey
- string login - User login name to enable.

Return Value

- int - 1 on success, exception thrown otherwise.

47.11 getCreateDefaultSystemGroup

Description

Returns the current value of the CreateDefaultSystemGroup setting. If True this will cause there to be a system group created (with the same name as the user) every time a new user is created, with the user automatically given permission to that system group and the system group being set as the default group for the user (so every time the user registers a system it will be placed in that system group by default). This can be useful if different users will administer different groups of servers in the same organization. Can only be called by an org_admin.

Parameters

- string sessionKey

Return Value

- int - 1 on success, exception thrown otherwise.

47.12 getDetails

Description

Returns the details about a given user.

Parameters

- string sessionKey
- string login - User's login name.

Return Value

- struct - user details

    - string "first_names" - deprecated, use first_name
    - string "first_name"
    - string "last_name"
    - string "email"
    - int "org_id"
    - string "org_name"
    - string "prefix"
    - string "last_login_date"
    - string "created_date"
    - boolean "enabled" - true if user is enabled, false if the user is disabled
    - boolean "use_pam" - true if user is configured to use PAM authentication

- boolean "read_only" - true if user is readonly
- boolean "errata_notification" - true if errata e-mail notification is enabled for the user

47.13 getLoggedInTime

Description

Returns the time user last logged in.

Deprecated - Never returned usable value.

Parameters

- string sessionKey
- string login - User's login name.

Return Value

- dateTime.iso8601

47.14 listAssignableRoles

Description

Returns a list of user roles that this user can assign to others.

Parameters

- string sessionKey

Return Value

- array:
  - string - (role label)

47.15 listAssignedSystemGroups

Description

Returns the system groups that a user can administer.

Parameters

- string sessionKey
- string login - User's login name.

Return Value

- array:

  - struct - system group

    - int "id"
    - string "name"
    - string "description"
    - int "system_count"
    - int "org_id" - Organization ID for this system group.

47.16 listDefaultSystemGroups

Description

Returns a user's list of default system groups.

Parameters

- string sessionKey
- string login - User's login name.

Return Value

- array:

  - struct - system group

    - int "id"
    - string "name"
    - string "description"

- int "system_count"
- int "org_id" - Organization ID for this system group.

47.17 listRoles

Description

Returns a list of the user's roles.

Parameters

- string sessionKey
- string login - User's login name.

Return Value

- array:

  - string - (role label)

47.18 listUsers

Description

Returns a list of users in your organization.

Parameters

- string sessionKey

Return Value

- array:

  - struct - user

    - int "id"
    - string "login"

- string "login_uc" - upper case version of the login
- boolean "enabled" - true if user is enabled, false if the user is disabled

47.19 removeAssignedSystemGroup

Description

Remove system group from the user's list of assigned system groups.

Parameters

- string sessionKey
- string login - User's login name.
- string serverGroupName
- boolean setDefault - Should system group also be removed from the user's list of default system groups.

Return Value

- int - 1 on success, exception thrown otherwise.

47.20 removeAssignedSystemGroups

Description

Remove system groups from a user's list of assigned system groups.

Parameters

- string sessionKey
- string login - User's login name.
- array:

  - string - serverGroupName
- boolean setDefault - Should system groups also be removed from the user's list of default system groups.

Return Value

- int - 1 on success, exception thrown otherwise.

47.21 removeDefaultSystemGroup

Description

Remove a system group from user's list of default system groups.

Parameters

- string sessionKey
- string login - User's login name.
- string serverGroupName

Return Value

- int - 1 on success, exception thrown otherwise.

47.22 removeDefaultSystemGroups

Description

Remove system groups from a user's list of default system groups.

Parameters

- string sessionKey
- string login - User's login name.
- array:

  - string - serverGroupName

Return Value

- int - 1 on success, exception thrown otherwise.

47.23 removeRole

Description

Remove a role from a user.

Parameters

- string sessionKey
- string login - User login name to update.
- string role - Role label to remove. Can be any of: satellite_admin, org_admin, channel_admin, config_admin, system_group_admin, or activation_key_admin.

Return Value

- int - 1 on success, exception thrown otherwise.

47.24 setCreateDefaultSystemGroup

Description

Sets the value of the CreateDefaultSystemGroup setting. If True this will cause there to be a system group created (with the same name as the user) every time a new user is created, with the user automatically given permission to that system group and the system group being set as the default group for the user (so every time the user registers a system it will be placed in that system group by default). This can be useful if different users will administer different groups of servers in the same organization. Can only be called by an org_admin.

Parameters

- string sessionKey
- boolean createDefaultSystemGruop - True if we should automatically create system groups, false otherwise.

Return Value

- int - 1 on success, exception thrown otherwise.

47.25 setDetails

Description

Updates the details of a user.

Parameters

- string sessionKey
- string login - User's login name.
- struct - user details

  - string "first_names" - deprecated, use first_name
  - string "first_name"
  - string "last_name"
  - string "email"
  - string "prefix"
  - string "password"

Return Value

- int - 1 on success, exception thrown otherwise.

47.26 setErrataNotifications

Description

Enables/disables errata mail notifications for a specific user.

Parameters

- string sessionKey
- string login - User's login name.
- boolean value - True for enabling errata notifications, False for disabling

Return Value

- int - 1 on success, exception thrown otherwise.

47.27 setReadOnly

Description

Sets whether the target user should have only read-only API access or standard full scale access.

Parameters

- string sessionKey
- string login - User's login name.
- boolean readOnly - Sets whether the target user should have only read-only API access or standard full scale access.

Return Value

- int - 1 on success, exception thrown otherwise.

47.28 usePamAuthentication

Description

Toggles whether or not a user uses PAM authentication or basic Satellite authentication.

Parameters

- string sessionKey
- string login - User's login name.
- int pam_value
    - 1 to enable PAM authentication
    - 0 to disable.

Return Value

- int - 1 on success, exception thrown otherwise.

48 user.external

If you are using IPA integration to allow authentication of users from an external IPA server (rare) the users will still need to be created in the Satellite database. Methods in this namespace allow you to configure some specifics of how this happens, like what organization they are created in or what roles they will have. These options can also be set in the web admin interface.

48.1 createExternalGroupToRoleMap

Description

Externally authenticated users may be members of external groups. You can use these groups to assign additional roles to the users when they log in. Can only be called by a satellite_admin.

Parameters

- string sessionKey
- string name - Name of the external group. Must be unique.
- array:

    - string - role - Can be any of: satellite_admin, org_admin (implies all other roles except for satellite_admin), channel_admin, config_admin, system_group_admin, or activation_key_admin.

Return Value

- struct - externalGroup

    - string "name"
    - array "roles"

- string - role

48.2   createExternalGroupToSystemGroupMap

Description

Externally authenticated users may be members of external groups. You can use these groups to give access to server groups to the users when they log in. Can only be called by an org_admin.

Parameters

- string sessionKey
- string name - Name of the external group. Must be unique.
- array:
  - string - groupName - The names of the server groups to grant access to.

Return Value

- struct - externalGroup
  - string "name"
  - array "roles"
    - string - role

48.3   deleteExternalGroupToRoleMap

Description

Delete the role map for an external group. Can only be called by a satellite_admin.

Parameters

- string sessionKey
- string name - Name of the external group.

Return Value

- int - 1 on success, exception thrown otherwise.

48.4 deleteExternalGroupToSystemGroupMap

Description

Delete the server group map for an external group. Can only be called by an org_admin.

Parameters

- string sessionKey
- string name - Name of the external group.

Return Value

- int - 1 on success, exception thrown otherwise.

48.5 getDefaultOrg

Description

Get the default org that users should be added in if orgunit from IPA server isn't found or is disabled. Can only be called by a satellite_admin.

Parameters

- string sessionKey

Return Value

- int - Id of the default organization. 0 if there is no default.

48.6 getExternalGroupToRoleMap

Description

Get a representation of the role mapping for an external group. Can only be called by a satellite_admin.

Parameters

- string sessionKey
- string name - Name of the external group.

Return Value

- struct - externalGroup

  - string "name"
  - array "roles"

    - string - role

48.7 getExternalGroupToSystemGroupMap

Description

Get a representation of the server group mapping for an external group. Can only be called by an org_admin.

Parameters

- string sessionKey
- string name - Name of the external group.

Return Value

- struct - externalGroup

  - string "name"
  - array "roles"

    - string - role

48.8 getKeepTemporaryRoles

Description

Get whether we should keeps roles assigned to users because of their IPA groups even after they log in through a non-IPA method. Can only be called by a satellite_admin.

Parameters

- string sessionKey

Return Value

- boolean - True if we should keep roles after users log in through non-IPA method, false otherwise.

48.9 getUseOrgUnit

Description

Get whether we place users into the organization that corresponds to the "orgunit" set on the IPA server. The orgunit name must match exactly the Satellite organization name. Can only be called by a satellite_admin.

Parameters

- string sessionKey

Return Value

- boolean - True if we should use the IPA orgunit to determine which organization to create the user in, false otherwise.

48.10 listExternalGroupToRoleMaps

Description

List role mappings for all known external groups. Can only be called by a satellite_admin.

Parameters

- string sessionKey

Return Value

- array:
  - struct - externalGroup

- string "name"
- array "roles"

    - string - role

48.11 listExternalGroupToSystemGroupMaps

Description

List server group mappings for all known external groups. Can only be called by an org_admin.

Parameters

- string sessionKey

Return Value

- array:

    - struct - externalGroup

        - string "name"
        - array "roles"

            - string - role

48.12 setDefaultOrg

Description

Set the default org that users should be added in if orgunit from IPA server isn't found or is disabled. Can only be called by a satellite_admin.

Parameters

- string sessionKey
- int defaultOrg - Id of the organization to set as the default org. 0 if there should not be a default organization.

Return Value

- int - 1 on success, exception thrown otherwise.

48.13 setExternalGroupRoles

Description

Update the roles for an external group. Replace previously set roles with the ones passed in here. Can only be called by a satellite_admin.

Parameters

- string sessionKey
- string name - Name of the external group.
- array:

    - string - role - Can be any of: satellite_admin, org_admin (implies all other roles except for satellite_admin), channel_admin, config_admin, system_group_admin, or activation_key_admin.

Return Value

- int - 1 on success, exception thrown otherwise.

48.14 setExternalGroupSystemGroups

Description

Update the server groups for an external group. Replace previously set server groups with the ones passed in here. Can only be called by an org_admin.

Parameters

- string sessionKey
- string name - Name of the external group.
- array:

  - string - groupName - The names of the server groups to grant access to.

Return Value

- int - 1 on success, exception thrown otherwise.

48.15   setKeepTemporaryRoles

Description

Set whether we should keeps roles assigned to users because of their IPA groups even after they log in through a non-IPA method. Can only be called by a satellite_admin.

Parameters

- string sessionKey
- boolean keepRoles - True if we should keep roles after users log in through non-IPA method, false otherwise.

Return Value

- int - 1 on success, exception thrown otherwise.

48.16   setUseOrgUnit

Description

Set whether we place users into the organization that corresponds to the "orgunit" set on the IPA server. The orgunit name must match exactly the Satellite organization name. Can only be called by a satellite_admin.

Parameters

- string sessionKey
- boolean useOrgUnit - True if we should use the IPA orgunit to determine which organization to create the user in, false otherwise.

Return Value

- int - 1 on success, exception thrown otherwise.

49 virtualhostmanager

Provides the namespace for the Virtual Host Manager methods.

49.1 create

Description

Creates a Virtual Host Manager from given arguments

Parameters

- string sessionKey - Session token, issued at login
- string label - Virtual Host Manager label
- string moduleName - the name of the Gatherer module
- parameters parameters - additional parameters (credentials, parameters for virtual-host-gatherer)

Return Value

- int - 1 on success, exception thrown otherwise.

49.2 delete

Description

Deletes a Virtual Host Manager with a given label

Parameters

- string sessionKey - Session token, issued at login
- string label - Virtual Host Manager label

Return Value

- int - 1 on success, exception thrown otherwise.

49.3 getDetail

Description

Gets details of a Virtual Host Manager with a given label

Parameters

- string sessionKey - Session token, issued at login
- string label - Virtual Host Manager label

Return Value

- struct - virtual host manager

  - string "label"
  - int "org_id"
  - string "gatherer_module"
  - struct "configs"

49.4 getModuleParameters

Description

Get a list of parameters for a virtual-host-gatherer module. It returns a map of parameters with their typical default values.

Parameters

- string sessionKey - Session token, issued at login
- string moduleName - The name of the module

Return Value

- map

49.5 `listAvailableVirtualHostGathererModules`

Description

List all available modules from virtual-host-gatherer

Parameters

- string sessionKey - Session token, issued at login

Return Value

- array:

  - string - moduleName

49.6 `listVirtualHostManagers`

Description

Lists Virtual Host Managers visible to a user

Parameters

- string sessionKey - Session token, issued at login

Return Value

- array:

  - struct - virtual host manager

    - string "label"
    - int "org_id"
    - string "gatherer_module"
    - struct "configs"

Colophon

This documentation is written in DocBook (see http://www.docbook.org ⌐). The XML source files were validated by **xmllint**, processed by **xsltproc**, and converted into XSL-FO using a customized version of Norman Walsh's stylesheets. The final PDF is formatted through XEP from RenderX. The open source tools and the environment used to build this manual are available in the package daps. The project's home page can be found at http://daps.sf.net/ ⌐.